First World War
and Army of Occupation
War Diary
France, Belgium and Germany

24 DIVISION
17 Infantry Brigade,
Brigade Trench Mortar Battery
16 March 1916 - 30 September 1918

WO95/2209/2

The Naval & Military Press Ltd
www.nmarchive.com
Published in association with The National Archives

Published by

The Naval & Military Press Ltd

Unit 10 Ridgewood Industrial Park,

Uckfield, East Sussex,

TN22 5QE England

Tel: +44 (0) 1825 749494

www.naval-military-press.com

www.nmarchive.com

This diary has been reprinted in facsimile from the original. Any imperfections are inevitably reproduced and the quality may fall short of modern type and cartographic standards.

Contents

Document type	Place/Title	Date From	Date To
Heading	WO95/2209/2		
Heading	17th Lt Trench. Mortar Bty Mar 1916-Sept 1918		
War Diary	G 11d 52	16/03/1916	18/03/1916
War Diary	Trenches, Sheet 28. I 18.d)	19/03/1916	21/03/1916
War Diary	28g. 13d.	21/03/1916	21/03/1916
War Diary	Eeke	22/03/1916	31/03/1916
War Diary	T28 b.6.10.	01/04/1916	11/04/1916
War Diary	(Sheet 28. T28 b 610. (TM Camp.	11/04/1916	23/04/1916
War Diary	Camp. T 28 b 610. Trenches. U14b 95.	24/04/1916	27/04/1916
War Diary	U14 b 95.	27/04/1916	28/04/1916
War Diary	Camp.T28b610 Trenches U14 b 9.5.	29/04/1916	30/04/1916
Heading	17th Light Trench Mortar Battery June 1916 Sep1918		
War Diary	Trenches 128 to 135 Opposite Messimes	01/06/1916	24/06/1916
War Diary	Sheet 28.	25/06/1916	25/06/1916
War Diary	S1d10.8.	26/06/1916	30/06/1916
Heading	17th Light Trench Mortar Battery July 1916		
Miscellaneous	To/The Officer A/c A.G's Office. The Base.	29/08/1916	29/08/1916
Heading	War Diary of 17th Light Trench Mortar Battery 24th Division From 1st July 1916 To 31st July 1916		
War Diary	Sheet 28 N 36 a & C	01/07/1916	20/07/1916
War Diary	Sheet 28 S.1.d.6.8	21/07/1916	22/07/1916
War Diary	Sheet 36 A F.5.e. 3.6	23/07/1916	24/07/1916
War Diary	Le Gard Farm	25/07/1916	31/07/1916
War Diary	Appendix 1	04/07/1916	04/07/1916
War Diary	Sheet 28 N. 36.a.3.7.	11/07/1916	11/07/1916
Miscellaneous	Appendix 3	17/07/1916	17/07/1916
Miscellaneous	Appendix 4	19/07/1916	19/07/1916
War Diary	Bainghem Le Comte	01/07/1917	16/07/1917
War Diary	Watterdal.	17/07/1917	17/07/1917
War Diary	Bayenghem. Lez Seninghem	18/07/1917	18/07/1917
War Diary	Map Reference No. 27/T.9.d.8.3.	19/07/1917	19/07/1917
War Diary	Caestre. Area. V.6.A.8.2.	20/07/1917	20/07/1917
War Diary	Eecke Area. Q.20.c.95.85	21/07/1917	21/07/1917
War Diary	Steenvoorde Area, K.26.c.20.15.	22/07/1917	25/07/1917
War Diary	Micmac Camp. F Camp.	25/07/1917	28/07/1917
War Diary	Micmac Camp.	30/07/1917	30/07/1917
War Diary	Rodkin House.	31/07/1917	31/07/1917
Heading	War Diary of 17th L.T.M. Battery For August 1917.		
War Diary	Rudkin Nee Tunnel 1.24.C.05.15. Sheet 28 Zillebeke	01/08/1917	03/08/1917
War Diary	Micmac Camp. H.31.d.40.80.	03/08/1917	06/08/1917
War Diary	Dickebusch H.34.A.20.70 Sheet. 28.N.W. Rudkin Hoode	07/08/1917	07/08/1917
War Diary	Tunnels. 1.24c.05.15 Sheet 28.N.1d.	08/08/1917	11/08/1917
War Diary	Micmac Camp H.31.D.40.80.	11/08/1917	12/08/1917
War Diary	Micmac Camp.H.31.D.40.80. Sheet 28. N.W.	13/07/1917	14/07/1917
War Diary	Dickebusch H. "O" Camp.	15/07/1917	15/07/1917
War Diary	H.28.D.9.7. Sheet. 28. N.W.	15/08/1917	18/08/1917
War Diary	Larch. Wood. 1.29.C. 20.50 Sheet. 28.Zillebeke	19/08/1917	23/08/1917
War Diary	Micmac Camp F H. 31.d. 40.80.Sheet 28.N.W.	24/08/1917	26/08/1917
War Diary	Dickebusch. "O".Camp. H.28. D.97 Sheet. 28. N.W.	27/08/1917	30/08/1917

War Diary	Larchwood 1.29.c.20.50	31/08/1917	31/08/1917
Heading	17th L.T. M.B Vol From Sept 1st-Sep 30th		
War Diary	Larch Wood Sheet 28.	01/09/1917	02/09/1917
War Diary	Micmac Camp "F" H 31 A. 6.5 Sheet 28	03/09/1917	05/09/1917
War Diary	Micmac Camp F H 31 A. 6.5	06/09/1917	07/09/1917
War Diary	Dickebusch 'O' H 28d 7.7. Sheet 28	08/09/1917	10/09/1917
War Diary	Menin Rd Tunnels Zillebeke	11/09/1917	15/09/1917
War Diary	Merris. Area Oultersteene. Hazebruck 5 A	16/09/1917	19/09/1917
War Diary	Oultersteene	20/09/1917	20/09/1917
War Diary	Bus. O 30 B-8.9 Sheet 57 C	21/09/1917	26/09/1917
War Diary	Haut-Allines	27/09/1917	27/09/1917
War Diary	C. 29b 2.4 Sheet 62	28/09/1917	28/09/1917
War Diary	Bernes-Montigny F F K 35b 5.7 Sheet 62 C	29/09/1917	30/09/1917
Heading	War Diary 17th Light Trench Mortar Battery Vol 4 October 1917		
War Diary	Sheet 62 C W E Montigny Farm K 35 B 50.70	01/10/1917	23/10/1917
War Diary	Montigny Farm K 35 B 50.70 Sheet 62 C.W.E.	11/10/1917	31/10/1917
Heading	War Diary of 17th Light Trench Mortar Battery for November 1917 Volume5		
War Diary	Montigny Farm Sheet 62 NE K 35 B 57	01/11/1917	11/11/1917
War Diary	Bernes 62 SE Q 10 a 10.80	15/11/1917	30/11/1917
Operation(al) Order(s)	72nd Infantry Brigade Operation Order No 192	16/11/1917	16/11/1917
Miscellaneous	Programme Of Artillery Support For Raid "A"		
Miscellaneous	Amendment & Addendum To 72nd Infantry Brigade Operation Order No. 192.	18/11/1917	18/11/1917
Heading	War Diary of 17 Light Trench Mortar Battery for the month of December 1917		
War Diary	Bernes 62 N.E.	01/12/1917	01/12/1917
War Diary	Le Verquier 62 B N.W. L 33d	02/12/1917	03/12/1917
War Diary	Dragoon Post 62 C N.W.G 31d. 90.70	03/12/1917	06/12/1917
War Diary	Hancourt 62q N E G 7b 1.2.	07/12/1917	17/12/1917
War Diary	Templeux. Le Gerard 62c NE L 2 B 90.10	18/12/1917	19/12/1917
War Diary	Hargicourt D.G. Positions. 62 C N.E. L 4 C 90.50.	19/12/1917	27/12/1917
War Diary	Templeux Le-Gerard 62E L28 90.10	28/12/1917	31/12/1917
Miscellaneous	8th Buffs	20/12/1917	20/12/1917
Miscellaneous	Table shewing "Battle Positions" to be occupied by supports. Reserves and Details in Brigade Area in event of Alarm or on receipt of Code word "Hot" from Bde H.Qrs		
Operation(al) Order(s)	17th Infantry Brigade Operation Order No 210	16/12/1917	16/12/1917
Miscellaneous	Relief Table "A" Issued with 17th Bde O.O. No. 619.		
Heading	War Diary of 17th Light Trench Mortar Battery for month of January 1918		
War Diary		01/01/1918	05/01/1918
War Diary	Hervilly Map. 62c K. 23d. 80.60	05/01/1918	13/01/1918
War Diary	Templeux. Map Ref Hargicourt Special Sheet L 2b. 90.05	13/01/1918	14/01/1918
War Diary	Hussar Post. Map Ref. Hargicourt Special Sheet L29b 5a. 15	15/01/1918	15/01/1918
War Diary	Map Ref Hargicourt S.M. Hargicourt L 5.c. 90.70.	16/01/1918	20/01/1918
War Diary	Hancourt Map. Ref 62 C. P.8.b.30.30.	21/01/1918	28/01/1918
War Diary	Hancourt Map Ref 62. Q. P.3.a.b.	29/01/1918	30/01/1918
War Diary	Hesbecourt. Map. 62C L B.C.	30/01/1918	31/01/1918
Operation(al) Order(s)	17th Infantry Brigade Operation Order No 215. Appendix 1	10/01/1918	10/01/1918

Miscellaneous	Table "A" to Accompany 17th Infantry Brigade O.O. No. 415		
Operation(al) Order(s)	17th Infantry Brigade Operation Order No 218 Appendix II	18/01/1918	18/01/1918
Operation(al) Order(s)	17th Infantry Brigade Operation Order No 219 Appendix III	18/01/1918	18/01/1918
Miscellaneous	Table "A" issued with 17th I. Bde O.O. 219		
Miscellaneous	Appendix IV	28/01/1918	28/01/1918
Heading	War Diary of the 17th Light Trench Mortar Battery February 1918	28/02/1918	28/02/1918
War Diary	Hancourt 62c S.E. Q 8b	01/02/1918	06/02/1918
War Diary	Roisel 62c. K. 16	07/02/1918	15/02/1918
War Diary	Templeux. Hargicourt Special	15/02/1918	15/02/1918
War Diary	Hervilly 62c. E 10b.	15/02/1918	28/02/1918
War Diary	Bernes. 62c S.E. Q.10.b	28/02/1918	28/02/1918
Heading	War Diary of 17th Light Trench Mortar Battery for April 1918		
War Diary	Fouencamps	01/04/1918	19/04/1918
War Diary	Ostreville	20/04/1918	30/04/1918
Heading	War Diary of 17th Light Trench Mortar Battery for May 1918.		
War Diary	Ostreville	01/05/1918	02/05/1918
War Diary	Sheet Lens 36c S H 1 Les Brebis	03/05/1918	13/05/1918
War Diary	Site S. Pierqe M 12b 25.5.	14/05/1918	20/05/1918
War Diary	Sheet Lens 36c.S.H. Cite S. Pierre	20/05/1918	29/05/1918
War Diary	Cite S Pierre	29/05/1918	29/05/1918
Heading	War Diary of 17th L.T.M. Battery, for June 1918.		
War Diary	North of Lens.	01/06/1918	30/06/1918
Heading	War Diary of 17th Light Trench Mortar Battery for July 1918		
War Diary	M12b20.60	01/07/1918	31/07/1918
Heading	War Diary of 17th Light Trench Mortar Battery for August 1918 Volume XIV		
War Diary	Sheet 44 Lens. (Cite. S. Pierre Battery H.9) Line	01/08/1918	05/08/1918
War Diary	Line	06/08/1918	31/08/1918
Heading	War Diary of 17th. Light Trench Mortar Battery Volume No. XV September 1918.		
Miscellaneous			
War Diary	In The Line	01/09/1918	17/09/1918
War Diary	Les Brebis.	17/09/1918	30/09/1918

24TH DIVISION
17TH INFY BDE

17TH LT TRENCH MORTAR BTY

~~JUN~~ MAR 1916-SEP 1918

Instructions regarding War Diaries and Intelligence Summaries are contained in F. S. Regs., Part II. and the Staff Manual respectively. Title pages will be prepared in manuscript.

WAR DIARY
or
~~INTELLIGENCE SUMMARY.~~
(Erase heading not required.)

Army Form C. 2118.

17/1 Trench Mortar Batty

Place	Date	Hour	Summary of Events and Information	Remarks and references to Appendices
G11 d 52.	16.3.16.		17/1 Trench Mortar Battery formed (25 men and 1 officer) after the men had been trained by the Officer Commanding Trench Mortar Batteries 24 Division.	
			Roll of Officers and men.	
			Lieut W. Asprey 3/The Buffs. Officer Commanding.	
			13936. Sgt Handford. J. 7488 Cpl Woodhead S. 10325 L/C Wright F.A. 15432. L/C Stacey A 10667. L/C Dannazy A	
			15339. L/C Flynn. 10456. Pte Bellringer. W. 15392. Pte Barton. A. 7992 Pte Burrell. H. 15012 Pte Cook T	
			9693. Pte Cunnold. A. 7334 Pte Colsel. H. 7881 Pte Douglas. M. 15178 Pte Fairall. J. 12201 Pte Garner J.	
			9523. Pte Harrington T 12474. Pte Hall G. 12396. Pte Ives G. 14109. Pte Noakes W 10911 Pte Papworth. C.	
			16910. Pte Redhead F 10955 Pte Sheppard. C. 11681. Pte Shatty. A. 8184 Pte Welsh. E 15866. Pte Webb. J.	
			All men of 1st Royal Fusilier Regt.	
	17.3.16.		Two 3.7 inch and two Stokes guns 136 3.7 in ammunition 130 rounds Stokes ammunition taken over by battery.	
	18.3.16.		Kit inspection. Preparation to enter trenches next day.	
Trenches. Sheet 28. I 18 d	19.3.16		1 Cpl and 6 men with 2 Stokes guns and two 3.7 inch enter trenches at Sanctuary Wood (Sheet 28 / I 18 d.) Right Stokes gun position in B3 to fire on Birdcage about 350 yds. Gun piece kept at junction of Grafton Street, and the Loop. Remainder of guns in reserve in Lovers Lane 400 yds from front line trench.	
	20.3.16.		2nd Stokes position commenced in Support Trench (Gordon Road) behind B1 to fire on Birdcage at range 360 yds	

T2134. Wt. W708—776. 500000. 4/15. Sir J. C. & S.

2/

Instructions regarding War Diaries and Intelligence Summaries are contained in F. S. Regs., Part II. and the Staff Manual respectively. Title pages will be prepared in manuscript.

WAR DIARY

or

~~INTELLIGENCE SUMMARY.~~

(Erase heading not required.)

Army Form C. 2118.

Place	Date	Hour	Summary of Events and Information	Remarks and references to Appendices
	20.3.16. Continued		Chief difficulty found in making emplacement was to form a solid base, so that base plate should not sink when gun was fired.	
	21.3.16		2nd Stokes position continued and finished. Some grenades were thrown over by enemy, but damage done nil. Enemies snipers were very active. One sniper sniping from Birdcage wounded four men of the Infantry before he could be removed. Infantry did not wish to use trench mortars in removing him so did not fire.	
28 S.13 d.			Orders received from 17th I.B. H.qrs to remove mortars from the trenches after dark 21st inst. 3.7 in ammunition 136 rounds and all detonated Stokes 45 rounds to be handed over to Canadian trench mortars taking over. Battery to be attached to 12 Royal Fusiliers to 12 Royal Fusiliers for rations, and to billet at Labour camp G 13 d between Vlamertinghe and Ouderdom. Relief complete 11 pm.	
	22.3.16		Orders received from 17 I.B. for guns and ammunition to be loaded on motor lorry by 6 pm. One man	
Eeke.			to travel with lorry. The battery was to proceed to Eeke on 23.3.16 Position on line of march behind 12 Royal Fusiliers. And to billet with No 3 company 12 Royal Fusiliers at end of march during rest period.	
	23.3.16.		Battery proceeds as per orders arriving in Billets (farm house) about 5 pm.	
	24.3.16.		Orders from 24th division via 17 Bge. Two stokes guns and ammunition to start at 6.30 am to be lent to	

T2134. Wt. W708—776. 500000. 4/15. Sir J. C. & S.

3/

Instructions regarding War Diaries and Intelligence Summaries are contained in F. S. Regs., Part II. and the Staff Manual respectively. Title pages will be prepared in manuscript.

WAR DIARY

or

~~INTELLIGENCE SUMMARY.~~

(Erase heading not required.)

Army Form C. 2118.

Place	Date	Hour	Summary of Events and Information	Remarks and references to Appendices
	24.3.16 continued		3rd Division. Delivered at Trench motor dump 3rd Division Dickebusch H33b by motor lorry about 10 a.m. No battery personnel were required with guns.	
			Two chaplains Capt Picton and Capt Lowry attached for boarding and rations. Monsieur Léon Belgian interpreter also attached for boarding and rations.	
	26.3.16		7.15. Physical Drill. 9.0 a.m. Squad Drill. 10 a.m. Semaphore parade.	
	25.3.16		7.15 Physical Drill 9.0 a.m Kit inspection 10 a.m Semaphore parade.	
	27.3.16		Officer commanding battery proceeds by motor bus to new area to inspect billets and trenches.	
	28.3.16		Orders received from 17 Bde. to send on party to take over new set of billets on 29.3.16.	
	29.3.16		Orders from 17 I Bde. to proceed to new area on 30 inst under battery arrangements. Advance party took over billets which were found to be in a disgracefully dirty condition. Also old equipment was scattered all over the place.	
	30.3.16		Battery proceeds to new area billets T28 b 6 10, arriving 4-30 p.m. Guns and kit were transferred by motor lorry. Battery attached to Machine Gun company for rations.	
	31.3.16.		Camp fatigues to clean and drain camp.	

[signature] Capt.

O.C. 17/1 Trench Mortar Bty. 24 Division

T2134. Wt. W708—776. 500000. 4/15. Sir J. C. & S.

4

Instructions regarding War Diaries and Intelligence Summaries are contained in F. S. Regs., Part II. and the Staff Manual respectively. Title Pages will be prepared in manuscript.

WAR DIARY
or
INTELLIGENCE SUMMARY
(Erase heading not required.)

Army Form C. 2118.

Place	Date	Hour	Summary of Events and Information	Remarks and references to Appendices
T28 b.6.10.	1.4.16		Battery not required to go into action except in one place. i.e. Opposite German Sap head on Ash Road (Sheet 28 U14 b 8. Not able to get the necessary range with 3.7 guns except here on Brigade front. Fatigues for cleaning camp & huts continued.	
	2.4.16		Drainage and other camp fatigues continued.	
	3.4.16		Camp fatigues.	
	4.4.16		Battery detailed for work at 17. S.B. Hqs on drains.	
	5.4.16		" " " " " " " "	
			No 11681. Pte Shale A. admitted to hospital.	
	6.4.16		Work finished at 17 S.B Hqs. 10456 Pte W. Bellringer proceeds on leave.	
	7.4.16		Camp drainage fatigues.	
	8.4.16		" " "	
	9.4.16		One 3.7 in gun ordered to be put in position and trained on German Sap Head on the Ash Road U14 b 8.	
	10.4.16		Dugout for men and gun position built U14 b 84. Camp Drainage Fatigues.	
	11.4.16		One corporal and two men with fatigue party to take gun and ammunition proceed to trenches. Gun put in position and trained on Sap head range 300 yds. Corporal has orders	

2449 Wt. W14957/M90 750,000 1/16 J.B.C. & A. Forms/C.2118/12.

5/

Instructions regarding War Diaries and Intelligence Summaries are contained in F. S. Regs., Part II. and the Staff Manual respectively. Title Pages will be prepared in manuscript.

WAR DIARY
or
INTELLIGENCE SUMMARY
(Erase heading not required.)

Army Form C. 2118.

Place	Date	Hour	Summary of Events and Information	Remarks and references to Appendices
Sheet 28. T.28 b 6.10. (T M Camp.			that he is not to fire unless he has orders from the Battery commander or is urgently requested by Trench commander. If possible he is to fire 3 rounds when medium trench mortars are firing to obtain the correct range. In case he has to retire, he will do so via Trend lane if possible. Get his gun into position up this trench so as to be able to support counter attack on trenches taken.	
	12.4.16		Situation normal in trenches. Camp fatigues continued	
	13.4.16		Two Stokes guns returned from 9th Division. Several parts missing including clinometers. Party in trenches slightly shelled about eleven o'clock in the morning over trench 128 & 129 with whizbangs and over 131 with 4.2 howitzers. Two men of battalion in trenches wounded. 9693 Pte A. Cunnold proceeds on leave.	
	14.4.16		Alternative position for 3.7 inch gun commenced. This work had to be done at night as men working during the day would be visible from the Messines ridge. Slight shelling in afternoon between 3 & 5 p.m. No damage done. Gun team relieved 9.0 a.m. Camp fatigues continued.	
	15.4.16		Situation normal. Camp fatigues continued.	

2449 Wt. W14957/M90 750,000 1/16 J.B.C. & A. Forms/C.2118/12.

6

Army Form C. 2118.

Instructions regarding War Diaries and Intelligence Summaries are contained in F. S. Regs., Part II. and the Staff Manual respectively. Title Pages will be prepared in manuscript.

WAR DIARY
or
INTELLIGENCE SUMMARY
(Erase heading not required.)

Place	Date	Hour	Summary of Events and Information	Remarks and references to Appendices
[illegible]	16.4.16.		Alternative position for 8.7 inch gun continued after dark. 130 & 131 lightly shelled about 2 p.m.	
	17.4.16.		Slight shelling with Whiz Bangs at dusk.	
	18.4.16		Situation normal.	
	19.4.16.		Situation normal.	
	20.4.16.		Trench relief. 2 direct hits on 132 between 10 am & 10.30 am	
	21.4.16		130/1 and Only Way whiz banged at 11 a.m. Also 128 and Anton's farm during the afternoon. Trench 130 & Seaforth farm were lightly shelled about 1 p.m. Camp work. Physical drill 7.15 each morning	
		11 pm	Gas alert.	
	22.4.16		Trenches 130 & 131 also Seaforth Farm shelled at 12.30 p.m.	
		11 p.m.	Gas alert cancelled.	
	23.4.16		Trenches 128 & 129 shelled 8.30 to 9.0 a.m. Seaforth farm & 130 shelled between 1.15 & 1.45 p.m. Trench mortars of small type fired on 132 & 133 between 9.30 p.m & 11.30 p.m. Very many more observation ~~[illegible]~~ balloons than normally were noticed. Trench relief.	

Instructions regarding War Diaries and Intelligence Summaries are contained in F. S. Regs., Part II. and the Staff Manual respectively. Title Pages will be prepared in manuscript.

WAR DIARY
or
INTELLIGENCE SUMMARY
(Erase heading not required.)

Army Form C. 2118.

Place	Date	Hour	Summary of Events and Information	Remarks and references to Appendices
Camp. T28b610. Trenches. U14b95.	24.4.16		Situation normal. Very slight shelling on 130. Alternative 3.7 in Gun position finished	
			Camp Work 7-15 AM Physical Drill 9-0 AM Fatigues at Bge HQs. 20 Fuser Respirators issued	
	25.4.16.		130, 131, and Only Way shelled during afternoon.	
	26.4.16		Trench relief 9-0 a.m. Slight shelling on 130 about 4 p.m. 12 Grenades on 127 at 2.30 p.m.	
			In Camp New Bomb store commenced.	
	27.4.16	1-15 am.	Gas alarm. All horns blown for some way round.	
			Copy of part of translation for a memorandum issued by French HQs on the lessons to be learnt from the fighting at Verdun	
			Defensive arrangements affecting the Infantry. Cover. Shelters are only of value if the occupants rely on being really safe from heavy shell fire, and can get out of them in time to meet an attack. To render shelters bomb proof against a heavy bombardment they are best made in the form of tunnelled galleries strutted and roofed with timber or by other means, and with at least 16 ft of solid earth over them. To enable the occupants to get out of them to meet an attack a sentry must be posted close to the shelter in a blinded observation post. These posts must be concealed, the parapet disguised and provided with an underground entrance. The sentry must have means of communication with the occupants of the shelter to give the alarm, and in case these should fail he must be able to get rapidly from	

2449 Wt. W14957/M90 750,000 1/16 J.B.C. & A. Forms/C.2118/12.

8/

Instructions regarding War Diaries and Intelligence Summaries are contained in F. S. Regs., Part II. and the Staff Manual respectively. Title Pages will be prepared in manuscript.

WAR DIARY
or
INTELLIGENCE SUMMARY

(Erase heading not required.)

Army Form C. 2118.

Place	Date	Hour	Summary of Events and Information	Remarks and references to Appendices
	27.4.16 Continued		the sentry post to the shelter to warn the occupants himself. To give the occupants time to get out ere should the enemy appear in the trenches simultaneously with the warning. Blockhouse traverses must be provided at suitable places in the trenches permitting of enfilade fire from loopholes along them. In addition to sentries, periscopes must be installed at carefully selected points in the line, so arranged so as to be capable of being used by observers in underground shelters. When there is any reason to anticipate an attack, Officers and N.C.Os must remain with their men in shelters. Shelters should be capable of accomodating from a squad to half a section. At least two, and if possible three exits should be provided. The incline down to the entrance must not be too steep. It can be made either in the form of a mine gallery open at the top or a stairway with lined sides. Entrenching tools, and grenades and rockets for warning the rear lines must be left in each shelter.	
			Lines of wire entanglement must be constructed some distance from trenches, and need not be continuous, so making it more difficult for enemy's artillery to register, and also giving it an increased area to be searched.	

2449 Wt. W14957/M90 750,000 1/16 J.B.C. & A. Forms/C.2118/12.

Instructions regarding War Diaries and Intelligence Summaries are contained in F. S. Regs., Part II. and the Staff Manual respectively. Title Pages will be prepared in manuscript.

WAR DIARY
or
INTELLIGENCE SUMMARY

(Erase heading not required.)

Army Form C. 2118.

Place	Date	Hour	Summary of Events and Information	Remarks and references to Appendices
	27.4.16 continued		Wire further from trenches to be put up first to keep enemy at distance should he use the Flammenwerfer in the attack. Trenches should be continuous. Observers in all trenches whether advanced, first, or second lines to give warning to their comrades, give the signal for barrage fire to be opened or repeat signals made by troops in front, and for this purpose should be provided with rockets. At all costs communication trenches must be numerous and deep to the rear. Every man must be trained to dig a sap, and should be able to tunnel.	
U14 b 95.			130 shelled about 5.30 p.m. More sniping than usual over 128 & 127.	
	28.4.16		Enemies sap head along Ash road pushed forward seventy to eighty yards. Apparently by means of tunnelling. Two 2 ind guns of 24th Battery and our 3.7 gun remain trained on sap. This probably is where sniping is carried on from the last two days as German trenches opposite 128 are in parts almost out of sight, and impossible to use for sniping. Searchlight used on Ash road. Unable to tell if used in sap or further behind.	

2449 Wt. W14957/M90 750,000 1/16 J.B.C. & A. Forms/C.2118/12.

W/

Instructions regarding War Diaries and Intelligence Summaries are contained in F. S. Regs., Part II. and the Staff Manual respectively. Title Pages will be prepared in manuscript.

WAR DIARY
or
INTELLIGENCE SUMMARY

(Erase heading not required.)

Army Form C. 2118.

Place	Date	Hour	Summary of Events and Information	Remarks and references to Appendices
Camp T28b6.10 Trenches U14b9.5	29.4.16		Relief carried out during morning. Secret orders received. i.e. In case of a sudden move forward the following personnel will be required for salvage purposes. 1 Other rank. On necessity arriving each unit will collect all stores in its possession at a convenient store or dump. The map reference of the dump selected and a note as to whether it is a barn etc; or hut will be forwarded to reach this office. Instructions with reference to above will be issued later. Signed Staff Captain 17th Infantry Bde. Place selected hut in camp T28b6.10. No L/C Stacey to be acting Corporal to complete establishment. 2/Lieut G. D. Stephens 1st Royal Fusiliers will be attached to 17/1 T M Bty and should join the battery by 12 midday April 30th. Situation normal.	
	30.4.16		Practice with Boxes respirators carried out every day. Situation normal.	

[signature] Capt.
OC 17/1 Trench Mortar Bty

2449 Wt. W14957/M90 750,000 1/16 J.B.C. & A. Forms/C.2118/12.

L 17th Brigade.
24th Division

17th LIGHT TRENCH MORTAR BATTERY

JUNE 1916

1 Sep 1918

Instructions regarding War Diaries and Intelligence Summaries are contained in F. S. Regs., Part II. and the Staff Manual respectively. Title Pages will be prepared in manuscript.

WAR DIARY
or
~~INTELLIGENCE~~ SUMMARY

(Erase heading not required.)

Army Form C. 2118.

17 T M Bty

Vol 3

Place	Date	Hour	Summary of Events and Information	Remarks and references to Appendices
Trenches 128 to 135.	1.6.16.		Fatigue party as usual working all night on repairing trench to new position.	
Opposite	2.6.16.		Work as 1st inst with extra fatigue party from 1st Royal Fusiliers of 8 men.	
Messines			9.7 Gun taken out of action from 128 trench was not thought necessary. Regiments in trenches relieved.	
	3.6.16.		A Trench Mortar fired on 132 at 1 P.M. Aerial Torpedoes were fired on 134/5 at 11-30 p.m.	
	4.6.16.		4 Stokes mortars received, to be handed over to 17/2 Battery on being formed.	
	~~[illegible]~~		Trench Mortars and aerial torpedoes fired on 134/5 at 5-30 p.m.	
	5.6.16.		Trench Mortar fired on 134/5 at 3 p.m.	
	6.6.16.		25 Trench Mortars on 134/5 at 12-30 a.m.	
	7.6.16.		Personnel of battery relieved	
	8.6.16.		5 Trench mortars fired on 135 at 7-30 p.m.	
	9.6.16.		A few aerial torpedoes fired on 134/5 at 9-30 p.m.	
	10.6.16		30 Trench mortars fired on 134/5 at 3-30 a.m. A few at 132 which fell short.	
			8 Buffs and 1st Royal Fusiliers relieve 9 Rifle Brigade and ~~[illegible]~~ 12 Royal Fusiliers	
	11.6.16.		Trench Mortars inactive.	

2449 Wt. W14957/M90 750,000 1/16 J.B.C. & A. Forms/C.2118/12.

Instructions regarding War Diaries and Intelligence Summaries are contained in F. S. Regs., Part II. and the Staff Manual respectively. Title Pages will be prepared in manuscript.

WAR DIARY
or
INTELLIGENCE SUMMARY

(Erase heading not required.)

Army Form C. 2118.

Place	Date	Hour	Summary of Events and Information	Remarks and references to Appendices
	12.6.16		Trench mortars inactive.	
	13.6.16.		Trench mortars inactive.	
	14.6.16.		Trench mortars inactive. Work on new positions and trenches continuing nightly. Nights so short that very often not more than three to four hours of working time.	
	15.6.16.		We fired 25 Stokes bombs from a temporary position made in 132 trench on to the Petit Douve. Medium trench mortars fired 9 sixty pounder bombs on front trench to right of Petit Douve. Germans retaliated with Whizz Bangs, a few 4.2 shells, and trench mortars on 132 & 133. Trench mortars could not get the range on 132. Some bombs falling 80 yds short. Flash of trench mortar reported U8 a 10.7.	
	16.6.16		17/1 & 17/2 Battery formed into one battery under the ~~name~~ title of 17th Trench Mortar Battery. Gas was sent over from 11-45 pm to 12-15 am by Germans. One man No 4008 Pte Broman of Buffs attached to the battery was slightly gassed. Through a faulty P.G. Helmet he was wearing, it is believed. Gas was thick at billets also (T28b610). Heavy bombardment by our guns during gas probably stopped attack. Gas was of a new type and very strong. Whistles were blown all down the line before being sent over.	
	17.6.16		Gas alert.	

2449 Wt. W14957/M90 750,000 1/16 J.B.C. & A. Forms/C.2118/12.

Army Form C. 2118.

WAR DIARY
or
~~INTELLIGENCE SUMMARY~~
(Erase heading not required.)

Instructions regarding War Diaries and Intelligence Summaries are contained in F. S. Regs., Part II. and the Staff Manual respectively. Title Pages will be prepared in manuscript.

Place	Date	Hour	Summary of Events and Information	Remarks and references to Appendices
	18.6.16		Gas alarm during night proved to be small quantities of gas shells fired on division on night. Gas alert cancelled.	
	19.6.16		Gas alert. Quiet day.	
	20.6.16		Gas alert cancelled. Quiet day.	
	21.6.16		Trench relief of Battery personnel. Canadian light trench mortar battery commander came to see trenches with a view to taking over.	
			Extract from 17th Brigade Order No 46 Copy 6.	
			The 2nd Australian Brigade will relieve the 17th Infantry Brigade in the Right Section trenches of the 24 Division area as follows:—	
			5. All details of relief will be arranged between O'sC Battalions, Trench Mortar Batteries and MG Companies of 17th Infantry Brigade and Second Australian Brigade. —	
			Rifle Grenades fired on Bosh Barriers in retaliation in proportion about 8 to 1.	
	22.6.16		Extract from 17th Infantry Brigade order No 47 Copy No 6.	
			Reference Brigade order No 46, the relief will take place as follows	
			(1) 24th June 2nd Australian Light Trench Mortar Battery relieves 17th Trench Mortar Bty 17th Light Trench Mortar Battery moves into Billets at Sheet 28 S1d10.8.	
			(3) All trench stores will be handed over to the relieving units of 2nd A Bge.	
			A list of stores handed over will be forwarded to Bge HQs	

2449 Wt. W14957/M90 750,000 1/16 J.B.C. & A. Forms/C.2118/12.

Instructions regarding War Diaries and Intelligence Summaries are contained in F. S. Regs., Part II. and the Staff Manual respectively. Title Pages will be prepared in manuscript.

Army Form C. 2118.

WAR DIARY
or
~~INTELLIGENCE SUMMARY~~
(Erase heading not required.)

Place	Date	Hour	Summary of Events and Information	Remarks and references to Appendices
	22.6.16	Continued	(4) Defence Schemes, Trench Maps, Log Books, Intelligence Reports, Tables of work in hand and proposed, and all documents and information which may be of value, will be handed over to relieving Battalions. A list of documents handed over will be sent to Brigade HQs. (5) Completion of relief will be reported to Brigade HQs by wiring "Your B.O. 47 complied with".	
	23.6.16		Situation Quiet.	
	24.6.16		Relief took place as 17th B.O. 47. about 11 p.m. Personnel relieved proceeded to billets T28 b 6.10 where it joined remainder of battery. Marching to rest area about 1 am next morning.	
Sheet 28.	25.6.16		Battery arrives in billets about 5.30 a.m.	
S.1.d.10.8.	26.6.16		Inspection of battery, cleaning of guns etc. Extract from 17th D B order No. 48 Copy 6. (3) The Brigade will be in Corps reserve. (5) Brigade HQs will be in house at M 29 c 2.6 immediately N.W. of church from 5 p.m 27th inst.	
	27.6.16		Battery drill and Gun drill.	

2449 Wt. W14957/M90 750,000 1/16 J.B.C. & A. Forms/C.2118/12.

Instructions regarding War Diaries and Intelligence Summaries are contained in F. S. Regs., Part II. and the Staff Manual respectively. Title Pages will be prepared in manuscript.

WAR DIARY
or
~~INTELLIGENCE~~ SUMMARY
(Erase heading not required.)

Army Form C. 2118.

Place	Date	Hour	Summary of Events and Information	Remarks and references to Appendices
	28.6.16.		Battery moved into billets at N30d28 Sheet 28. Brigade still in corps reserve.	
	29.6.16.		Extracts of 17th I.B. order No 50 Copy 6. (1) The Brigade will take over the front between the Wulverghem - Wytschaete Road at N36a71 and the Kemmel Wytschaete Road at N29b9½.6½. i.e. Trenches D5 to F5 both inclusive, in relief of one battalion 72nd and one battalion 73rd Infantry Brigades according to table attached. (2) All details of relief will be arranged between Battalion Commanders, O.C.s Machine Gun Coys and O.C.s Trench Mortar batteries concerned (3) All trench stores on the front taken over will be taken over. A list of trench stores taken will be forwarded to Brigade Headquarters. (4) Defence schemes, trench maps, log books, tables of work in hand and proposed, and all documents and information which may be of value will be taken over. A list of documents etc taken over will be forwarded to Brigade Hqrs (5) The command of the sector taken over will pass to B.G.C. 17th Infantry Brigade on completion of relief on the night of 1st/2nd July 1916. Extract from Table. Relief of 72 Trench Mortar Battery by 17th T.M. Bty will take place on 1.7.16. Exchange of billets will also take place on 1.7.16.	

2449 Wt. W14957/M90 750,000 1/16 J.B.C. & A. Forms/C.2118/12.

Instructions regarding War Diaries and Intelligence Summaries are contained in F. S. Regs., Part II. and the Staff Manual respectively. Title Pages will be prepared in manuscript.

WAR DIARY
or
~~INTELLIGENCE~~ SUMMARY
(Erase heading not required.)

Army Form C. 2118.

Place	Date	Hour	Summary of Events and Information	Remarks and references to Appendices
	29.6.16 continued		G H Q No O.B 1594. 2nd Army No F/326. V Corps No GX 6444. 24 Division No Q/4195. A new type of long range cartridges for the 3" Stokes Mortar has been received, in replacement of the old red Cartridge. The distinguishing mark of the new Cartridges is the red lead with which they are all provided. The cases are of different colours, but none are green. Their average extreme range is 420 yds. It must be noted that the graduations for red cartridges on the clinometer may not be quite accurate, at extreme ranges, for the new cartridges. Owing to the haste of production, the preparation of range tables for use with the new cartridges has not been possible, and probably it will not be necessary.	
			DGMD No S/565. 2nd Army No 104/4B. V Corps. No VQ/3682. Defects found in 3" Stokes mortar ammunition. (i) The seating in the shell which takes the detonator is not true to gauge, detonators do not fit in easily. (ii) Safety buttons too rough to allow of its free engagement on discharge from the fly off lever, thus causing blinds; buttons have also been found bent under the pressure exerted by the lever. (iii) The cartridge container bursts when used with the red cartridge.	
			Stand to 10.25 p.m cancelled 11.10 p.m. Heavy bombardment tonight.	

Army Form C. 2118.

Instructions regarding War Diaries and Intelligence Summaries are contained in F. S. Regs., Part II. and the Staff Manual respectively. Title Pages will be prepared in manuscript.

WAR DIARY
or
~~INTELLIGENCE~~ SUMMARY

(Erase heading not required.)

Place	Date	Hour	Summary of Events and Information	Remarks and references to Appendices
	29.6.16	continued	Copy of wire from H Q 29 Division. QMG wire begins QDS 4049/B 28th AAA. A Stokes bomb has been found having a hole leading direct from the cartridge container into the inside of the bomb AAA. Apparently a top guide with hole for copper gaine was used in place of the usual solid bottom guide AAA Such a bomb if fired would detonate in the mortar AAA. All 3" Stokes bombs must be examined before being used; to make certain that there is no hole leading from the cartridge container through the lower guide into the explosive filling the bomb AAA For this purpose a thin piece of wire or stick can be used ~~AAA~~. ends. AAA for immediate action. AAA.	
	30.6.16		New trenches to be taken over reconnoitred.	

2449 Wt. W14957/M90 750,000 1/16 J.B.C. & A. Forms/C.2118/12.

17th Brigade,
24th Division.

17th LIGHT TRENCH MORTAR BATTERY

JULY 1916.

To/ the Officer i/c A.G.'s Office.
The Base.

Herewith forwarded War Diary for July. Delay much regretted; due to death in action of O.C. battery, and the exigencies of active service.

T.A.R. Barnard Lieut.
29/8/16 O.C. 14th Trench Mortar Batt.

24 July

Vol 4

17. T M B

CONFIDENTIAL

WAR DIARY

OF

17TH LIGHT TRENCH MORTAR BATTERY

24TH DIVISION

FROM 1ST JULY 1916 TO 31ST JULY 1916

Army Form C. 2118.

Instructions regarding War Diaries and Intelligence Summaries are contained in F. S. Regs., Part II. and the Staff Manual respectively. Title Pages will be prepared in manuscript.

WAR DIARY
~~or~~
~~INTELLIGENCE SUMMARY~~

(Erase heading not required.)

Place	Date	Hour	Summary of Events and Information	Remarks and references to Appendices
Sheet 28 N 36 a & c	1.7.16	5 p.m.	Trenches taken over from left sector of 72nd Brigade and right sector of 73rd Brigade. Three gun positions ~~in~~ south of WULVERGHEM – WYTSCHAETE road in support trench N.36.c.8.9. Three positions north of road N.35.b.10.5 and N.36.a.2.5 (two positions).	Battery H.Q. at N.31.d.8.8 (8-inch farm).
		10 p.m.	Half the personnel of battery enter the trenches. Relief was carried out directly after dark and was entirely satisfactory, except for one man slightly wounded in the neck.	
			Quiet day. Enemy fired a few trench mortars on Bull-Ring (N.30.c.3.1).	
ditto	2.7.16		Very quiet day. Positions improved.	
ditto	3.7.16		Quiet day. Headcover constructed.	
ditto	4.7.16		Quiet day.	
ditto	5.7.16	11 p.m.	Bombardment commenced by our artillery. Retaliation by whizzbangs, trench mortars, minenwerfer, and 220-pounders; enemy used hardly any heavy artillery. This battery fired 166 rounds south of road and 25 from forward position north of road. One man slightly wounded in the shoulder by shrapnel.	
ditto	6.7.16	12.30 a.m.	Bombardment slackened	
		1 a.m.	Bombardment ceased. Intermittent enemy retaliation with heavy mortars continued for about an hour. Remainder of the day quiet.	
			Received notes from 2nd Army on use of Stokes Mortars in bombing attacks.	Appendix 1

2449 Wt. W14957/M90 750,000 1/16 J.B.C. & A. Forms/C. 2118/12.

Instructions regarding War Diaries and Intelligence Summaries are contained in F. S. Regs., Part II. and the Staff Manual respectively. Title Pages will be prepared in manuscript.

WAR DIARY

~~or INTELLIGENCE SUMMARY~~

(Erase heading not required.)

Army Form C. 2118.

Place	Date	Hour	Summary of Events and Information	Remarks and references to Appendices
Sheet 28 N.36.a & c	6.7.16 (cont.)		17th I.B. order No. 51 copy 6 received:— "8th Buffs will be relieved by 3rd Rifle Brigade on night of 8th/9th after dark. 1st R.F. " " " 12th R.F. " " " " " " "	
ditto.	7.7.16	8p.m.	Medium T.M. Battery fired 16 bombs behind Spanbroekmolen (N.30.c.2.8). Enemy replied with 12 minenwerfers (rum-jars), employing 2 mortars.	
ditto	8.7.16	11a.m.	A few heavy trench mortars fired by enemy about N.29.d.9.5. Retaliation on Spanbroekmolen with 60-pounders.	
			17th I.B. order No. 52 copy 6 received:— "Ref. 17th I.B. order No. 51, relief of 1st R.F. by 12th R.F. cancelled. Following relief will take place tonight July 8th/9th: 12th R.F. will relieve a battalion of the 7th Australian Brigade in trenches C4 to D4 inclusive (U.1.b.1.4 to N.36.a.5.1)."	
ditto	9.7.16	5a.m.	2/Lieut. G.D. STEPHENS killed by a sniper, whilst looking over the parapet at N.36.a.8.1. Normal activity throughout the day.	
ditto	10.7.16		Quiet day. 17th I.B. order No. 53 received:— "9th Royal Sussex (73rd I.B.) will relieve 12th R.F. in trenches C4 to D4 inclusive tonight July 10th/11th."	

2449 Wt. W14957/M90 750,000 1/16 J.B.C. & A. Forms/C.2118/12.

Army Form C. 2118.

Instructions regarding War Diaries and Intelligence Summaries are contained in F. S. Regs., Part II. and the Staff Manual respectively. Title Pages will be prepared in manuscript.

WAR DIARY

or

~~INTELLIGENCE SUMMARY~~

(Erase heading not required.)

Place	Date	Hour	Summary of Events and Information	Remarks and references to Appendices
Sheet 28 N.36.a+c.	10.7.16 (cont.)	5 p.m.	Our mortars north of WULVERGHEM-WYTSCHAETE road relieved by 73rd T.M. Battery. Mortars removed to reserve dugouts behind 1st R.F. in left sector of Brigade front (N.35.b.) ready to be put into action.	
ditto	11.7.16	1 a.m.	A raid on enemy trenches made by a party of the 3rd Rifle Brigade, from a point slightly to right of the Bull-Ring (about N.36.a.3.7) for purposes of identification.	Appendix 2 Details of raid and notes.
			17th I.B. order No. 54 Copy 6 received:— "12th R.F. will relieve 1st R.F. in left sub-sector on night of 13th/14th July."	
ditto	12.7.16	9.30 a.m.	Enemy fired 5 Trench Mortars, all short of trench D5.	
		5 p.m.	Medium T.M. Battery fired 5 ranging shots. Were searched for ineffectually by enemy whizzbangs.	
ditto	13.7.16		Quiet day. 3 other ranks joined for duty.	
			17th I.B. order No. 55 Copy 6 received:— "8th Buffs will relieve 3rd R.B. in right sub-sector on night of 15th/16th July."	
ditto	14.7.16		Quiet day.	
ditto	15.7.16	11 a.m.	2/Lieut. W.H. TEMPLE, 8th Buffs. reported for duty.	

2449 Wt. W14957/M90 750,000 1/16 J.B.C. & A. Forms/C.2118/12.

Army Form C. 2118.

Instructions regarding War Diaries and Intelligence Summaries are contained in F. S. Regs., Part II. and the Staff Manual respectively. Title Pages will be prepared in manuscript.

WAR DIARY

~~INTELLIGENCE SUMMARY~~

(Erase heading not required.)

Place	Date	Hour	Summary of Events and Information	Remarks and references to Appendices
Sheet 28 N.36.a+c.	15.7.16 (cont:)	12 noon	55 rounds fired in retaliation to enemy minenwerfer. During the action one gun and 97 rounds of ammunition were accidentally blown up, owing to a defective shell which started fusing as soon as the safety-pin was removed, and (no less) to the reprehensible conduct of the gunner handling it, who immediately dropped it in the gun emplacement, and (with two others) fled. No casualties.	
ditto	16.7.16		Quiet day.	
ditto	17.7.16	3 p.m.	2/Lieut. H. FRANKHAM SMITH, 12th R.F. joined for duty.	
			17th I.B. order No. 56 Copy 6 received, relating to a minor enterprise to be carried out by the 12th R.F. on the night 17th/18th July, in conjunction with gas + smoke.	Appendix 3 text of B.O.56
ditto	18.7.16	12.5 a.m.	Raid by 12th R.F. carried out. 14 Germans killed: no prisoners. Raiders lost one officer missing. No gas or smoke used, as wind unfavorable. T.M. Battery fired 280 rounds during artillery bombardment. Enemy retaliation confined entirely to minenwerfer; no artillery of any description employed.	
			17th I.B. order No. 57 received:— "No working parties to be in 17th I.B. area after 10.30 p.m. tonight 18th/19th July unless wind unfavorable for us to send over gas, as remainder of last night's scheme will be carried out as detailed for last night."	

2449 Wt. W14957/M90 750,000 1/16 J.B.C. & A. Forms/C.2118/12.

Instructions regarding War Diaries and Intelligence Summaries are contained in F. S. Regs., Part II. and the Staff Manual respectively. Title Pages will be prepared in manuscript.

WAR DIARY

~~or~~

~~INTELLIGENCE SUMMARY~~

(Erase heading not required.)

Army Form C. 2118.

Place	Date	Hour	Summary of Events and Information	Remarks and references to Appendices
Sheet 28 N.36.a+c.	18.7.16 (cont.)		The scheme, however, was again deferred, the wind being still unfavorable.	
ditto	19.7.16		17th I.B. order No. 58 received, ref. relief of 17th I.B. by 151st I.B.	Appendix 4 copy of B.O. 58
ditto	20.7.16	11a.m.	Battery relieved by 151st T.M.B. Party from trenches proceed to Battery H.Q. at N.31.d.8.8	
		11p.m.	Battery moves back to rest billets at Sheet 28 S.1.d.6.8. Move delayed by non-arrival of motor-lorry detailed to convey guns etc., which finally were loaded on 8 handcarts and dragged by hand. Balance of kit left behind in charge of 1 N.C.O and 2 men.	
Sheet 28 S.1.d.6.8	21.7.16		Battery in rest billets. Remainder of kit fetched from N.31.d.8.8.	
		4p.m.	17th Brigade H.Q. closes at Locre and opens at house on BAILLEUL-METEREN road, X.17.c.3.4.	
ditto.	22.7.16	12noon	Battery moved from billets at S.1.d.6.8. to farm at Sheet 36A F.5.c.3.6.	
Sheet 36A F.5.c.3.6	23.7.16		Complete rest for Battery.	
ditto	24.7.16	7a.m.	Battery left billets and marched to railway station at BAILLEUL, where it entrained.	

Army Form C. 2118.

Instructions regarding War Diaries and Intelligence Summaries are contained in F. S. Regs., Part II. and the Staff Manual respectively. Title Pages will be prepared in manuscript.

WAR DIARY

~~or~~

~~INTELLIGENCE SUMMARY~~

(Erase heading not required.)

Place	Date	Hour	Summary of Events and Information	Remarks and references to Appendices
	24.7.16	10.28a.m.	Train left BAILLEUL.	
	(cont.)	6.30p.m.	Train arrived AMIENS. Battery detrained. Kit loaded on motor-lorry. Personnel of Battery start to march to billets at Le Gard farm, 12 miles N.W. of AMIENS.	
LE GARD FARM	25.7.16	3a.m.	Personnel of Battery arrive at LE GARD FARM, after losing their way owing to the complete absence of any map of the locality.	
ditto	26.7.16		Battery trained in the advance	
ditto	27.7.16		Training continued.	
ditto	28.7.16		Battery split up into 4 parts; 2 teams with their guns being attached to each battalion in the Brigade. Officers and men as far as possible go to their own battalions.	
	29.7.16		Training with battalions in attack.	
	30.7.16		Trench Mortars in attack. Two methods attempted:- (1) advance with rear platoon of attacking company - not considered satisfactory (2) kept in reserve at convenient place until required - better, but not altogether good; ammunition supply very difficult.	
	31.7.16		Battery moves with battalions by train to Sheet 62D K.18.a, BOIS DE TAILLES.	

2449 Wt. W14957/M90 750,000 1/16 J.B.C. & A. Forms/C.2118/12.

Instructions regarding War Diaries and Intelligence Summaries are contained in F. S. Regs., Part II. and the Staff Manual respectively. Title Pages will be prepared in manuscript.

WAR DIARY
or
~~INTELLIGENCE SUMMARY~~

(Erase heading not required.)

Army Form C. 2118.

Place	Date	Hour	Summary of Events and Information	Remarks and references to Appendices
			Appendix 1.	
	4.7.16		Notes from 2nd Army on the use of Stokes Mortars in Bombing Attacks.	
			1. Whenever possible Stokes Mortars should be used to assist bombers.	
			2. They should be so placed that they can bring a concentrated and continuous fire on a point previously fixed in the enemy's trench about 50 yards beyond the length to be secured by the bombers.	
			3. The position of the mortars may be either in the trench from which the bombing raid is made, so as to give enfilade fire, or in our own trenches opposite the objective. A combination of frontal and enfilade fire should be employed whenever possible.	
			4. The following points should be attended to by Stokes Mortar officer:—	
			(i) The target should be carefully ranged on before the operation commences.	
			(ii) Fire should be opened at the moment of attack and continued until the piece of trench gained is consolidated.	
			(iii) A plentiful supply of ammunition should be at the mortars before the attack is undertaken.	

Army Form C. 2118.

WAR DIARY

~~INTELLIGENCE SUMMARY~~

(Erase heading not required.)

Instructions regarding War Diaries and Intelligence Summaries are contained in F. S. Regs., Part II. and the Staff Manual respectively. Title Pages will be prepared in manuscript.

Place	Date	Hour	Summary of Events and Information	Remarks and references to Appendices
			Appendix 1 (continued)	
			5. The Stokes Mortar can also be used to fire ahead of bombers as they proceed down the trench, but this method should only be employed when observation is so favorable that the Stokes Mortar officer can make certain that he can follow the movements of the bombers down the trench.	

2449 Wt. W14957/M90 750,000 1/16 J.B.C. & A. Forms/C.2118/12.

Army Form C. 2118.

WAR DIARY
or
~~INTELLIGENCE SUMMARY~~

(*Erase heading not required.*)

Instructions regarding War Diaries and Intelligence Summaries are contained in F. S. Regs., Part II. and the Staff Manual respectively. Title Pages will be prepared in manuscript.

Place	Date	Hour	Summary of Events and Information	Remarks and references to Appendices
			Appendix 2	
			Details of raid by 3rd R.B. on 11/7/16, and Notes.	
Sheet 28 N.36.a.3.7.	11.7.16	1a.m.	Our artillery opened fire, putting barrage on enemy support line. Raiding party entered enemy front line.	
		1.10a.m.	Raiding party returned to their own trenches. A multi-coloured rocket sent up as signal to artillery to drop on to enemy front line. Our trench mortars opened on seeing this signal, and fired 72 rounds on front line.	
			Enemy retaliation confined mainly to trench mortars, only two field-gun batteries and one 4.2-inch battery being observed to fire. Shelling was heaviest round the Bull-Ring (N.36.a.3.7). Our artillery destroyed one enemy trench mortar.	
			The following notes are made:—	
			1. The present system of bomb squads is efficient.	
			2. The Germans run from their front line to their second, and also open fire from their second; this points to a surprise attack being essential.	
			3. Enemy attempted no bombing or counter-attack.	

2449 Wt. W14957/M90 750,000 1/16 J.B.C. & A. Forms/C.2118/12.

Instructions regarding War Diaries and Intelligence Summaries are contained in F. S. Regs., Part II. and the Staff Manual respectively. Title Pages will be prepared in manuscript.

WAR DIARY

~~or~~

~~INTELLIGENCE SUMMARY~~

(Erase heading not required.)

Army Form C. 2118.

Place	Date	Hour	Summary of Events and Information	Remarks and references to Appendices
			Appendix 2 (continued)	
			4. Dugouts are of very much the same pattern as those made by our R.Es., and are put up under the front parapet.	
			5. The trenches were about 7 ft. deep, revetted with wire and expanding metal, and paved with duckboards.	
			6. Communication trench was winding, U framed in places, but without duckboards and without traverses.	
			7. The parapet was good.	
			8. Two bays were without firesteps.	
			9. Wire was very deep and nearly touched parapet, but was no serious obstacle with mats.	

Instructions regarding War Diaries and Intelligence Summaries are contained in F. S. Regs., Part II. and the Staff Manual respectively. Title Pages will be prepared in manuscript.

WAR DIARY

~~or~~

~~INTELLIGENCE SUMMARY~~

(Erase heading not required.)

Army Form C. 2118.

Place	Date	Hour	Summary of Events and Information	Remarks and references to Appendices
			Appendix 3	
	17.7.16		Copy of 17th I.B. order No. 56	
			1. A minor enterprise will be carried out by the 12th Royal Fusiliers on the night of 17th/18th July against SPANBROEKMOLEN (N.30.c) according to scheme submitted by O.C. 12th R.F.	
			2. Gas and smoke will be discharged from the 17th I.B. front (provided the wind is favourable) according to time-table attached.	
			3. O.C. 8th Buffs will decide whether gas is to be let off from trenches D3 and D6, or not. The officer K company R.E. in those trenches will give the necessary expert advice.	
			4. A gap will be left in the smoke cloud through which the raiding party will advance. O.C. 12th R.F. will decide where the gap is to be left.	
			5. Zero time will be notified on the afternoon of 17th July.	
			6. There will be no artillery bombardment prior to 0.02 min.	
			(continued)	

2449 Wt. W14957/M90 750,000 1/16 J.B.C. & A. Forms/C.2118/12.

Army Form C. 2118.

Instructions regarding War Diaries and Intelligence Summaries are contained in F. S. Regs., Part II. and the Staff Manual respectively. Title Pages will be prepared in manuscript.

WAR DIARY
or
~~INTELLIGENCE SUMMARY~~

(Erase heading not required.)

Place	Date	Hour	Summary of Events and Information	Remarks and references to Appendices

Appendix 3 (continued)

7. Zero time will be the moment at which the raiding party enters enemy trench.
8. At 1 hour 20 minutes after Zero time patrols of 8th Buffs will enter German trenches at about N.36.a.5½.3 and N.36.a.5.8½ to ascertain the effect of the gas; to be arranged with O.C. 12th R.F.

Trench Mortars will fire 75 yards each side of raiding party on front trench when artillery bombardment commences.

B.O. §177. There will be no working parties on the 17th I.B. area tonight 17th/18th July.

Time Table of events during raid:—

Zero – Gas starts. Raiding party enters German trenches.
0.2 min. – Smoke starts. Artillery and Stokes Mortar bombardment.
0.9 min. – Gas stops.
0.30 min. – Smoke stops.

2449 Wt. W14957/M90 750,000 1/16 J.B.C. & A. Forms/C.2118/12.

(continued)

Army Form C. 2118.

Instructions regarding War Diaries and Intelligence Summaries are contained in F. S. Regs., Part II. and the Staff Manual respectively. Title Pages will be prepared in manuscript.

WAR DIARY
or
~~INTELLIGENCE SUMMARY~~

(*Erase heading not required.*)

Place	Date	Hour	Summary of Events and Information	Remarks and references to Appendices
			Appendix 3 (continued)	
			1 hour 0 min. – 2nd bombardment of enemy front line at selected points by 24th Divisional Artillery, Trench Mortars, and Stokes Guns.	
			1 hour 20 min. – Smoke discharged along 24th Division front. Artillery lifts to enemy 2nd line. Our troops opposite points bombarded (i.e. U.2.a.2.5 and N.3.d.7½.1) cheer. Patrols 8th Buffs advance to enemy trenches.	
			1 hour 22 min. – Artillery return to front line at selected points (excluding points entered by 8th Buffs).	
			1 hour 45 min. – Artillery cease. Smoke ceases.	

2449 Wt. W14957/M90 750,000 1/16 J.B.C. & A. Forms/C.2118/12.

Instructions regarding War Diaries and Intelligence Summaries are contained in F. S. Regs., Part II. and the Staff Manual respectively. Title Pages will be prepared in manuscript.

WAR DIARY
or
~~INTELLIGENCE SUMMARY~~
(Erase heading not required.)

Army Form C. 2118.

Place	Date	Hour	Summary of Events and Information	Remarks and references to Appendices
			Appendix 4.	
	19.7.16		Copy of 17th I. B. order No. 58.	
			1. The Brigade will be relieved by the 151st I. B. on 19th and 20th July, as per table attached. All arrangements will be made between Battalion Commanders, Machine Gun Commanders, and Light T. M. Battery Commanders concerned.	
			2. All trench stores will be handed over to relieving units. A record of stores handed over will be kept by brigades.	
			3. Defence schemes, log books, etc. will be handed over to relieving units. A list of documents handed over will be forwarded to Brigade.	
			4. Stokes Mortars will be withdrawn from the line; ammunition will be handed over.	
			5. Command of sector will pass to B. G. C. 151st I. B. on completion of reliefs on the night of 19th/20th July.	
			6. No discharge of gas will take place on nights of 19th/20th or 20th/21st July. The arrangements for messages to be sent from Divisional H.Q. at 3 p.m. daily	

2449 Wt. W14957/M90 750,000 1/16 J.B.C. & A. Forms/C.2118/12.

Instructions regarding War Diaries and Intelligence Summaries are contained in F. S. Regs., Part II. and the Staff Manual respectively. Title Pages will be prepared in manuscript.

WAR DIARY

~~or~~

~~INTELLIGENCE SUMMARY~~

(Erase heading not required.)

Army Form C. 2118.

Place	Date	Hour	Summary of Events and Information	Remarks and references to Appendices
			Appendix 4 (continued).	
			until gas has been discharged, are cancelled.	
			7. Completion of reliefs will be reported to Brigade H.Q. by wiring N.C.C. three two six.	
			17th T.M. Battery will proceed to rest-area immediately after relief. Rest area to be notified later.	
			End of War Diary for July 1916.	
			(signed) F.H.B. Barnard Lieut. O.C. 17th Light T.M. Battery 24th Division	

2449 Wt. W14957/M90 750,000 1/16 J.B.C. & A. Forms/C.2118/12.

July 1917

Instructions regarding War Diaries and Intelligence Summaries are contained in F. S. Regs., Part II. and the Staff Manual respectively. Title Pages will be prepared in manuscript.

WAR DIARY

or

~~INTELLIGENCE SUMMARY~~

(Erase heading not required.)

Army Form C. 2118.

17th Light Trench Mortar Battery

Vol

Place	Date	Hour	Summary of Events and Information	Remarks and references to Appendices
BAINGHEM LE COMTE	1st		First Day in new Rest Billets at BAINGHEM LE COMTE. Complete day of rest. Weather bad, rained most of the day.	
	2nd		Another complete Rest-Day. Battery went for a Bathe in a Stream near Sanghem. Weather completely changed. Very fine & hot.	
	3rd		Another rest Day. Everything cleaned up & men refitted. Weather still being fine.	
	4th		Training started today. Working 6 hours a day & finishing at 3 p.m. Weather very unsettled. Periodical very heavy showers. Slightly hindered training.	
	5th		Weather unsettled in the morning but changed to clear & sunshine in afternoon. Training not interfered with.	
	6th		Training continued. Weather clear and warm. Revolver practice in morning.	
	7th		Still fine and warm, but rather cold at night. Training carried on as usual. Nothing special to record.	
	8th 9th		Heavy thunderstorm in early morning, clearing up later, but dull the whole day.	
	10th		Training continued. Dull but warm day. Nothing special to record.	
	11th		Field day from 8 A.M. to 4 P.M. Live shells fired. Good results. Training took place on high ground about 3 kilos N. E. of LICQUES.	
	12th		Training continued. The "Snipers" performed at 1st R. F. billets in evening. Greatly appreciated by battery. An officer arrived from 3rd R. B. to take command of battery. Inspection of battery by new C. O., after which [illegible] 6 hours [illegible]	
	13th		Lecture by G. S. O. 1. 6 officers and N. C. Os. proceeded to SENINGHEM to view model and [illegible] Brigade Sports held today. [illegible] Battery [illegible]	

2449 Wt. W14957/M90 750,000 1/16 J.B.C. & A. Forms/C.2118/12.

July 1917.

Instructions regarding War Diaries and Intelligence Summaries are contained in F. S. Regs., Part II. and the Staff Manual respectively. Title Pages will be prepared in manuscript.

WAR DIARY
or
~~INTELLIGENCE SUMMARY~~
(Erase heading not required.)

7th Light Trench Mortar Battery

Army Form C. 2118.

Place	Date	Hour	Summary of Events and Information	Remarks and references to Appendices
BAINGHEM-LE COMTE	14th		Heavy shower in morning which interfered slightly with training. [illegible] days training carried out today.	
	15th		This morning billets and stores were searched by a search party acting under orders of brigade for any motor bicycles which were unlawfully in possession. Nothing was found. We had to find search party to search M.G. billets. Weather fine and warm. No special training today.	
	16th		Battery went for a route march in the morning. For the remainder of the day there was the usual training. Men had baths in the afternoon. Weather fine and warm.	
WATTERDAL.	17th	5.15 AM.	Paraded and marched to WATTERDAL. Weather warm. In the afternoon the corps commander visited the officers of the battery.	
BAYENGHEM-LEZ SENINGHEM	18th	7.46 AM.	Paraded and marched to BAYENGHEM-LEZ-SENINGHEM. Officers and N.C.O.s of battery visited divisional model at SENINGHEM in the afternoon. Lecture on trench mortars for remainder of battery by B.S.M. Very wet the whole day.	
Map reference 27/T.9.D.8.3.	19th	2.45 AM.	Paraded and marched to farm at 27/T.9.D.8.3. Men were provided with hot meal before starting and had breakfasts en route at 6.0 AM, when whole brigade halted. Weather cloudy all day. Slight rain in early morning.	
CAESTRE AREA V.6.A.8.2.	20th	6.45 AM.	Paraded and marched to farm at V.6.A.8.2, where we remained for one night.	
EECKE AREA. Q.20.C.95.85	21st	6.30 AM	Paraded and marched to farm at Q.20.C.95.85. Gun drill and other training carried out during morning. Inspection of gas helmets, box respirators, and steel helmets in afternoon.	
STEENVOORDE AREA. K.26.C.20.15	22nd	6.AM.	Paraded and marched to K.26.C.20.15. Special training carried out here for the next few days. Visited by area commandant in morning, who gave us specially good billets.	

2449 Wt. W14957/M90 750,000 1/16 J.B.C. & A. Forms/C.2118/12.

July 1917

Instructions regarding War Diaries and Intelligence Summaries are contained in F. S. Regs., Part II. and the Staff Manual respectively. Title Pages will be prepared in manuscript.

WAR DIARY
or
~~INTELLIGENCE SUMMARY~~
(Erase heading not required.)

Army Form C. 2118.

7th Light Trench Mortar Battery

Place	Date	Hour	Summary of Events and Information	Remarks and references to Appendices
STEENVOORDE.	23rd		Training carried out special attention being paid to gun drill and gun firing. Successful results obtained. Experiments were carried out with green cartridge and two rings. Guns cleaned in afternoon, also shells. Cricket match afterwards with a company of 12th R. Fus.	
	24th		An officer from T.M.B with officers from other units of brigade going to ~~[illegible]~~ reconnoitre assembly positions for coming offensive and lines of approach. Ordinary day's training carried out. Visit of Archbishop of York in morning. In afternoon cricket match against H.Q. coy of 12th R. Fus.	
MICMAC CAMP. F CAMP.	25th	3.30 AM	Battery paraded and marched to F camp in MICMAC camp, having breakfasts en route. Slight shower about 7 A.M. which rather spoilt last part of march. Packs were carried in lorry which arrived in afternoon.	
	26th		Rifle and general equipment inspection. Inspection and test of box respirators by brigade gas N.C.O. Order read out on parade with regard to mustard oil gas.	
	27th		Inspection and box respirator practice. Order read out on parade with regard to new German gas, mustard oil gas. German aeroplane flies overhead at night. No casualties.	
	28th		Inspection and box respirator practice. German aeroplane overhead at night. A few bombs dropped.	
	29th	1 A.M.	Gas alarm. Message from Bde H.Q. saying suspicious of gas in back areas. Slight smell of gas but nothing else.	
		9.15 AM	Heavy thunderstorm. Church parade cancelled. Rain all day. Advanced party sent up to HEDGE St. Tunnels to look after rations.	

2449 Wt. W14957/M90 750,000 1/16 J.B.C. & A. Forms/C.2118/12.

July 1917.

Instructions regarding War Diaries and Intelligence Summaries are contained in F. S. Regs., Part II. and the Staff Manual respectively. Title Pages will be prepared in manuscript.

WAR DIARY
or
~~INTELLIGENCE SUMMARY~~
(Erase heading not required.)

17th Light Trench Mortar Battery

Army Form C. 2118.

Place	Date	Hour	Summary of Events and Information	Remarks and references to Appendices
MICMAC CAMP	30th		Guns and limber sent up to VALLEY COTTAGES in early morning as that is quietest part of day. Today is Y Day. Battery parades 1.30 P.M. and marches to old G.H.Q. line near CAFÉ BELGE. March to RUDKIN HOUSE continued about 5.30 P.M. Whole battery	
RUDKIN HOUSE			accomodated in tunnels in RUDKIN HOUSE. An officer reports to Bde H.Q. in HEDGE St. Tunnels at night for synchronisation of watches. Stokes guns not being used in the attack, the personnel being used as an ammunition carrying party under orders of staff captain.	
	31st	3.50 A.M.	Zero hour for attack. Battery not in action at all today. Several shells on top of tunnels during day but no damage done. Carrying party of 1 officer and 30 O.R. to take up ammunition to 12th R. F. at 6. P.M. Held up 6 hours by shell fire. Double journey had to be done. Work not finished till next morning.	

A E Price [illegible]
for O.C. 17th L.T.M.B.

2449 Wt. W14957/M90 750,000 1/16 J.B.C. & A. Forms/C.2118/12.

Instructions regarding War Diaries and Intelligence Summaries are contained in F. S. Regs., Part II, and the Staff Manual respectively. Title pages will be prepared in manuscript.

WAR DIARY
or
INTELLIGENCE SUMMARY.
(*Erase heading not required.*)

Army Form C. 2118.

Place	Date	Hour	Summary of Events and Information	Remarks and references to Appendices
			CONFIDENTIAL	
			WAR DIARY	
			OF	
			17th L.T.M. BATTERY.	
			FOR	
			AUGUST 1917.	
			VOLUME	
			[signature] Capt.	
			5. 9. 17	

D. D. & L., London, E.C.
(A7883) Wt W809/M1672 350,000 4/17 Sch. 52a Forms/C/2118/14

August 1917

Instructions regarding War Diaries and Intelligence Summaries are contained in F. S. Regs., Part II, and the Staff Manual respectively. Title pages will be prepared in manuscript.

WAR DIARY
or
~~INTELLIGENCE SUMMARY.~~

(Erase heading not required.)

17th Light Trench Mortar Battery

Army Form C. 2118.

Place	Date	Hour	Summary of Events and Information	Remarks and references to Appendices
RUDKIN HSE TUNNEL	1st		Battery finished yesterday's carrying party at 12 30 P.M. today. At 2 30 P.M. another carrying	
I.24.C.05.15. SHEET 28 ZILLEBEKE			party was ordered to take [illegible] up to 12th [illegible] H.Q. Delayed by shell fire. Finished at 9 P.M.	
			No casualties. Very heavy rain in morning and early part of afternoon.	
	2nd		No carrying party in morning. One ordered for 4 P.M. to take up S.A.A. to M.G. Coy's advanced H.Q.	
			Party suddenly cancelled till next morning. Heavy rain during most of the day.	
	3rd		Party starts at 4 A.M. with S.A.A. for M.G.C. 15 boxes were taken up. No casualties. Much finer	
			than preceding day, but slight drizzle at times. Directly party returns, guns and [illegible]	
			petrol tins are taken down to VALLEY COTTAGES dump to be picked up by limber in afternoon.	
MICMAC CAMP.			Orders to move back to MICMAC camp having come through. Battery immediately returns to	
H.31.D.40.80.			MICMAC arriving there at about 11 A.M., when it began to rain. No camp allotted to us till [illegible]	
			in the afternoon. Men each given a clean change at night.	
	4th	8AM	Baths for men at DICKEBUSCH. Two others men reported sick. On the whole not a high percentage.	
			Day spent in general cleaning up of everything. Showers at intervals during the day.	
	5th		Rifle inspection in morning. Much drier day. Sun shining for several hours.	
	6th		Rifle and general equipment inspection in morning. In afternoon the [illegible] occupied by us	
			[illegible] taken to form new camp in DICKEBUSCH. Battery followed later.	[illegible]

D. D. & L., London, E.C.
(A7883) Wt W8c9/M1672 350,000 4/17 Sch. 52a Forms/C/2118/14

August 1917

Instructions regarding War Diaries and Intelligence Summaries are contained in F. S. Regs., Part II. and the Staff Manual respectively. Title pages will be prepared in manuscript.

WAR DIARY
or
~~INTELLIGENCE SUMMARY.~~

17th Light Trench Mortar Battery

(*Erase heading not required.*)

Army Form C. 2118.

Place	Date	Hour	Summary of Events and Information	Remarks and references to Appendices
Dickebusch H.34.A.20.70. Sheet 28.N.W. Rudkin House	7th		Box respirators, iron ration and field dressing inspection before going up the line. 17th L.T.M. Battery [illegible] 72nd and 73rd [illegible] During night 7/8th Battery moves to Rudkin House tunnels, arriving there at about 2.[?] A.M. Tunnel found in filthy condition.	
Tunnels. I.24.C.05.15 Sheet 28.N.W.	8th		All day spent in cleaning out the tunnel and baling out as much water as possible. Thunderstorm in evening, which makes the tunnel leak in places, but not very much.	
"	9th		The entrance, which has been nearly blocked up for some time, is cleaned out during the day, and steps are made. A great improvement. The baling of water still continues in the absence of a pump, which cannot be obtained.	
"	10th		Morning of attack by part of division on our left. Urgent message came through in afternoon for a party of 1 officer and 20 O.R. to act as S.B. to 8th [?] Surreys in brigade on our left. Good work done and message of thanks received from M.O. of the regt. Party returned at about 6 A.M. next morning, being delayed by shell fire.	
	11th		Orders received for relief today by 73rd L.T.M. Battery. Battery goes down in small parties to	
Micmac Camp H.31.D.40.80.			Micmac Camp at 12 noon. No casualties in battery during tour in trenches. Weather fine till about 2 o'clock when heavy rain begins. 6 tents for battery and stores.	
"	12th		No church parade. Inspection in morning and general cleaning up. Weather fine except for occasional showers.	

[illegible]

D. D. & L., London, E.C. (A7883) Wt W8c9/M1672 50,000 4/17 Sch. 52a Forms/C/2118/14

August 1917

Instructions regarding War Diaries and Intelligence Summaries are contained in F. S. Regs., Part II. and the Staff Manual respectively. Title pages will be prepared in manuscript.

WAR DIARY
or
~~INTELLIGENCE SUMMARY.~~

(*Erase heading not required.*)

17th Light Trench Mortar Battery

Army Form C. 2118.

Place	Date	Hour	Summary of Events and Information	Remarks and references to Appendices
MICMAC CAMP H.31 D.40.80 Sheet 28. N.W	13th		Inspection and gun drill in morning. New 2nd Army gun drill carried out. One officer and 2 N.C.Os on 4 days' course of P.T. and B.F. Special instructor takes battery in afternoon from 2-3 P.M. in P.T. & B.F. 9 shelters and 6 tents taken over today instead of what we had	
"	14th		Inspection and gun drill in morning. PT in afternoon for an hour taken by special instructor. Occasional showers during day. Heavy rain during night	
DICKEBUSCH. "O" camp. H.28 D.9.7 Sheet. 28.N.W	15th		Battery moves to camp "O" near DICKEBUSCH where tents are taken over. Gun drill in morning. Bombs dropped in Dickebusch for an hour before battery arrived. During night enemy shelled heavily [illegible] above probably trying for 12" gun near camp. Another thunderstorm during afternoon.	
	16th		Rifle inspection in morning. Weather fine and warm. P.T. & B.F. in afternoon taken by army gymnastic instructor.	
	17th		Inspection and drill in morning. P.T. & B.F. in afternoon. Weather much finer on the whole.	
	18th		Inspection and drill and B.F. carried out during the morning. Also box respirator drill. Divisional guard round the camp during the morning. Rocket [illegible] demonstration in the morning by 17th & 73rd I.B. P.T. & B.F. in afternoon by gymnastic instructor. Weather fine and warm except few small showers.	
LARCH WOOD I.29 C.20.60 Sheet. 28. ZILLEBEKE	19th		17th Bde go into the line today and tonight relieving 72nd Bde. 1 officer and N.C.O. sent up in the morning to take over from 72nd L.T.M.B. Battery in LARCH WOOD. 10 guns in action. Relief in daylight.	
	20th		Battery placed at disposal of O.C. M.G.C. for carrying S.A.A. to forward dumps. Two journeys done which meant some very hard work. 1 off. 40 O.R. formed the party	

[signature]

D. D. & L., London, E.C. (A7883) Wt W809/M1672 350,000 4/17 Sch. 52a Forms/C/2118/14

August 1917.

Instructions regarding War Diaries and Intelligence Summaries are contained in F. S. Regs., Part II, and the Staff Manual respectively. Title pages will be prepared in manuscript.

WAR DIARY

or

~~INTELLIGENCE SUMMARY.~~

(*Erase heading not required.*)

17th Light Trench Mortar Battery

Army Form C. 2118.

Place	Date	Hour	Summary of Events and Information	Remarks and references to Appendices
LARCH WOOD	21st	12 noon	A Carrying party consisting of 1 officer and 20 O.R. at disposal of M.G.C. carried 2000 rds S.A.A. to front line [illegible]	
I.29.C.20.50. SHEET 28 ZILLEBEKE		3.30 P.M.	C.O. 2nd Lt Bishop and 1 N.C.O. sent to get German minenwerfer out of a position about 100 yds in front of right Batt H.Q. The C.O. was sent for to go to Bde H.Q. so that the job was not completed. C.O. reported at Bde H.Q. and was ordered to take two guns into action in conjunction with 1st R.F. at I.19.R.8.1. A carrying party of 1 officer & 60 O.R. from Buffs was sent for to carry Stokes ammunition to front line. C.O. went forward to reconnoitre strong point, returned to [illegible] at Tunnels to arrange details with C.O. 1st R.F. & then went to front line and reported to O.C. coy 1st R.F. who was arranging the raid	
	22nd	6 A.M.	Teams arrived in front line with their guns and immediately dug guns into position. Guns were mounted and ready to fire at 6.20 A.M. but owing to darkness and uncertainty of guide ammunition had not arrived.	
		6.10 A.M.	Ammo arrived. Hard work to get ready for firing at Z-5 but everything was ready at 6.50 A.M. at Z-7 (6.53 A.M.) registering shot was fired. Ranged correctly. At Z-5 fire opened with both guns at 4 rds per minute. Rate of fire was increased until at [illegible] maximum was reached, & fire maintained at 22 rds per minute, until Z+22 when assaulting party left the trench. Range increased 100 yds & 2nd objective fired on. Assaulting party took 1st obj: 85 prisoners & 1 Machine gun, with loss of only 1 man wounded. Great accuracy of fire obtained, nearly every shot being a direct hit. About 130 rds were fired during this action. The 2nd obj. was found to be unoccupied, but there was signs of recent occupation. The teams returned to Larch Wd at night, arriving soon after 10 P.M.	[signature]

D. D. & L., London, E.C. (A7883) Wt W8c9/M1672 250,000 4/17 Sch. 52a Forms/C/2118/14

August 1917

Instructions regarding War Diaries and Intelligence Summaries are contained in F. S. Regs., Part II, and the Staff Manual respectively. Title pages will be prepared in manuscript.

WAR DIARY
or
~~INTELLIGENCE SUMMARY.~~
(Erase heading not required.)

Army Form C. 2118.

7th Light Trench Mortar Battery

Place	Date	Hour	Summary of Events and Information	Remarks and references to Appendices
Larch Wood I.29.c.20.50. Sheet 28.N.W.	23rd		Orders for relief today came through. Relieving unit 73rd T.M.B. Now relieving officer having come up, and checking everything to hand over, the battery left [illegible] in 2 parties at about 3 P.M. and came to Micmac Camp. Heavy showers of rain, just before 2nd party arrived.	
Micmac Camp H.31.d.40.80. Sheet 28.N.W.	24th		General cleaning up today and usual training carried out. The [illegible] instructed in the [illegible]. Several showers during day. The [illegible] were to have given [illegible] an entertainment today, but owing to unfavourable weather, was postponed till Sunday.	
	25th		Rifle inspection and training carried out. Classes [illegible] held for attached men. Messages of congratulation from corps and divisional commanders on success of recent operation, in which battery was engaged, were read out to battery on parade this morning.	
	26th		No church parade today. Instead usual training carried out. No parade in afternoon. Heavy rainstorm in evening and most of the night.	
Dickebusch Camp H.28.d.9.7. Sheet 28.N.W.	27th		Gun firing carried out this morning, with 2 guns at ranges about 500 yds. Very successful results. Interesting and instructive to all ranks. Shells fired without [illegible]. Heavy rainstorm in early afternoon. Moved to Dickebusch Camp in afternoon. One officer sent on ahead to take over from 72nd Bde.	
	28th		Usual training programme carried out during morning as far as possible. Heavy rain during night and early morning, flooding the stream running alongside the camp. Strong wind blowing most of the day.	
	29th		Inspection and gun drill in morning. Fire drill carried out. In course of time this drill will become a [illegible]. Then men are put on to building sandbag wall round the tents 2 feet high, to stop splinters from a new [illegible] which has a most sensitive fuse. Work continued in afternoon. This is a divisional order.	[illegible initials]

D. D. & L., London, E.C. (A7883) Wt W8c9/M1672 50,000 4/17 Sch 52a Forms/C/2118/14

August 1917

Instructions regarding War Diaries and Intelligence Summaries are contained in F. S. Regs., Part II. and the Staff Manual respectively. Title pages will be prepared in manuscript.

WAR DIARY
or
~~INTELLIGENCE~~ SUMMARY.

(Erase heading not required.)

Army Form C. 2118.

17th Light Trench Mortar Battery.

Place	Date	Hour	Summary of Events and Information	Remarks and references to Appendices
DICKEBUSCH.	30th		Gun drill for an hour in the morning. Then work on sandbag walls continued.	
"O" camp			Box respirator drill and inspection in afternoon. Weather much finer though still	
H.28.d.9.7.			cold. Rain towards evening.	
LARCH WOOD	31st		Relieve 72nd T M B in the line. Two right hand guns taken over, which fire on	
I.29.c.20.60			LOWER STAR Post. Relief in afternoon.	[illegible]

H. J. Layton Capt.
O.C. 17th L.T.M.B.

D. D. & L., London, E.C.
(A7883) Wt W809/M1672 350,000 4/17 Sch. 52a Forms/C/2118/14

Instructions regarding War Diaries and Intelligence Summaries are contained in F. S. Regs., Part II. and the Staff Manual respectively. Title pages will be prepared in manuscript.

WAR DIARY
or
~~INTELLIGENCE SUMMARY.~~
(Erase heading not required.)

Army Form C. 2118.

Place	Date	Hour	Summary of Events and Information	Remarks and references to Appendices
			17th L.T.M.B.	
			Vol 5	
			From Sep 1st — Sep 30th	
			H.H. Layton Capt.	
			O.C. 17 L.T.M.B.	

D. D. & L., London, E.C.
(A7853) Wt W809/M1672 350,000 4/17 Sch. 52a Forms/C/2118/14

September 1917

Instructions regarding War Diaries and Intelligence Summaries are contained in F. S. Regs., Part II, and the Staff Manual respectively. Title pages will be prepared in manuscript.

WAR DIARY
or
INTELLIGENCE SUMMARY.
(*Erase heading not required.*)

Army Form C. 2118.

17th Light Trench Mortar Battery

Place	Date	Hour	Summary of Events and Information	Remarks and references to Appendices
LARCH WOOD Sheet 28	1st		The remainder of the battery which is in Larch Wood tunnels draw all the stokes shells from JACKSON'S DUMP and bring them to Larch Wood Dump where they are fuzed and detonated ready to be taken up to the gun positions. Relieving officer from 117th Bde came up in morning to take over. They are relieving us tomorrow. Guides etc are arranged.	Map ref. for I.29.c.2.0 Sheet 28. N.W.
	2nd		Receive orders that we are not to be relieved till tomorrow evening. In afternoon the two teams in the line and the officers are relieved for the 24 hours. Quiet whole of the while.	
MICMAC CAMP "F" H 31 A 6.5 Sheet 28	3rd		Several Boche aeroplanes over our lines in the morning, but no particular shelling takes place. The battery is relieved in the afternoon by 116th T.M.B (39th Div). Teams in the line relieved at about 5 P.M. Battery comes down to F Camp MICMAC. Several Boche aeroplanes came over at about 9 o'clock, but no bombs dropped near our camp.	H.31.d.4.0.8 Sheet 28 N.W.
	4th		General cleaning up today. Weather fine and warm. 1 officer and 1 N.C.O. sent to N.1.A. central for instruction in Bullet and bayonet practice.	
	5th		Special cleaning up for inspection by brigadier general. At the last minute inspection was postponed till tomorrow. Building walls round shelters and tents continued both morning and afternoon. Thunderstorm at night. Officers and N.C.Os go to range in afternoon for revolver shooting practice.	

Y E Barnwell 2Lt

D. D. & L., London, E.C. (A7883) Wt W8c9/M1672 750,000 4/17 Sch. 52a Forms/C/2118/14

September 1917

Instructions regarding War Diaries and Intelligence Summaries are contained in F. S. Regs., Part II, and the Staff Manual respectively. Title pages will be prepared in manuscript.

WAR DIARY
or
INTELLIGENCE SUMMARY.
(*Erase heading not required.*)

Army Form C. 2118.

9th Light Trench Mortar Battery

Place	Date	Hour	Summary of Events and Information	Remarks and references to Appendices
Micmac Camp A. H31 A 6.5	6th		Inspection by Divisional general in morning. We paraded with M.G.C. Wall building around tents continued, both morning and afternoon. Thunderstorm at night. Very close all day.	Sheet 28 N.W. H31 A.40.80
	7th		Wall building continued today. Moved to DICKEBUSCH camp in afternoon and take camp over from 72nd I.B.	
Dickebusch 6 H28 d 7.7 Sheet 28	8th		Parade in morning for inspection. Gun drill carried out for about an hour. Afterwards box respirator drill. Weather fine and warm.	H28 D.9.7.
	9th		Voluntary church parade in morning held in the camp. Splinter proof walls round tents continued in afternoon. No work on this job was done by preceding unit 72nd I.B. [illegible] netting and stakes used for one tent. Sandbags used for remainder.	
	10th		Inspection and then work on splinter proof walls continued. Weather fine and warm. Box respirators inspected by battery gas N.C.O.	

F.E. Barnwell 2Lt

D. D. & L., London, E.C. (A7883) Wt W809/M1672 350,000 4/17 Sch 52a Forms/C/2118/14

September 1917

Instructions regarding War Diaries and Intelligence Summaries are contained in F. S. Regs., Part II, and the Staff Manual respectively. Title pages will be prepared in manuscript.

WAR DIARY
or
INTELLIGENCE SUMMARY.
(Erase heading not required.)

7th Light Trench Mortar Battery

Army Form C. 2118.

Place	Date	Hour	Summary of Events and Information	Remarks and references to Appendices
MENIN RD TUNNELS ZILLEBEKE	11th		Relieving 72nd L.B. in the line opposite INVERNESS COPSE. Guides met at BIRR X roads on MENIN RD at 12 o'clock noon. Very quiet relief. 3 guns in the line, 1 in reserve in H.Q.	
	12th		An officer from 69th Bde comes up to look round today. We carry up ammunition to the two new battle positions made by 72nd Bde for the next attack. 60 boxes carried up today. They were stacked there in the boxes. Gas shells were sent over by the Boche in the very early hours of the morning. Gas helmets had to be worn in the tunnels.	
	13th		Orders received today from Division to make two forward dumps of Stokes ammunition, one in JASPER LANE and one in JASPER AVENUE, as far up each as possible. Dumps to be of 250 rounds and to be splinter proof. Shells carried up by infantry carrying party to CLAPHAM JUNCTION. From there, L.T.M.B. carried them up to the advanced dumps, where they were fused and detonated by the teams in the line.	
	14th		Work on the advanced dumps finished today. An officer expected to come up from relieving unit, 70th I.B., to look round, but he doesn't turn up. O.C. reports to Bde H.Q this afternoon at 4 P.M to talk over details with relieving unit. Relief orders received for tomorrow. Relief arranged for 12 noon.	
	15th		Corps have artillery barrage this morning at 8 A.M. Practice barrage.	

F.E. Barnwell 2Lt

D. D. & L., London, E.C.
(A7883) Wt W809/M1672 350,000 4/17 Sch. 52a Forms/C/2118/14

September. 1917

Instructions regarding War Diaries and Intelligence Summaries are contained in F. S. Regs., Part II, and the Staff Manual respectively. Title pages will be prepared in manuscript.

WAR DIARY
or
INTELLIGENCE SUMMARY.
(Erase heading not required.)

Army Form C. 2118.

7th Light Trench Mortar Battery

Place	Date	Hour	Summary of Events and Information	Remarks and references to Appendices
	15th		Boche became very active after this and swept the tracks with whizzbangs whenever he saw anyone walking about. Relieving units got a lot of trouble. Nevertheless they arrive up safely. Our battery reaches VICKSBURG "O" camp about 5 P.M. Another practice barrage at 4 P.M.	
MERRIS area OULTERSTEENE Hazebrouck 5A	16th		Bde moving by buses to MERRIS area. Very early start in the morning. Eventually arrive about 10.30 A.M. Find good billets. Expect to be here for a few days. Football kicked about during the afternoon. Weather quite warm, the sun being out for several hours.	
	17th		Parades in the morning for P.T. and B.F. and squad drill with and without arms. General cleaning up in the afternoon. After parades in morning the men were taken to baths.	
	18th		Parades in morning for P.T. & B.F. and squad drill and lecture on the gun and new gun drill as it was raining. Football match in afternoon against two companies of the Buffs. Smoking concert at night. Great success.	
	19th		Inspection by new divisional general, Major-General Daly. Complimented a smart and clean turnout. Class of attached men taken in gun drill by Sgt. Storey. Football match in afternoon against M.G.C.	

J E Barnwell 2lt

D. D. & L., London, E.C.
(A7883) Wt W8c9/M1672 250,000 4/17 Sch. 52a Forms/C/2118/14

September 1917

Instructions regarding War Diaries and Intelligence Summaries are contained in F. S. Regs., Part II. and the Staff Manual respectively. Title pages will be prepared in manuscript.

WAR DIARY
or
INTELLIGENCE SUMMARY.
(*Erase heading not required.*)

9th Light Trench Mortar Battery

Army Form C. 2118.

Place	Date	Hour	Summary of Events and Information	Remarks and references to Appendices
OUTTERSTEENE	20th		Lorry to take stores etc. to BAILLEUL STATION (WEST) arrived at about 11 A.M. Morning taken up loading up all limbers and G.S. wagon, also handcarts. Parade at 7.15 P.M. to march to the station arriving there at 8.15, 3 hours before train is due to start. An officer was sent on ahead in morning to take over camp near BAPAUME. Train loaded up very quickly.	Ref. Map
BUS O30 G 8.9 Sheet 57 C	21st		Arrived in BAPAUME (WEST) station at about 9 A.M. Tea served out at Church Army hut in BAPAUME. Afterwards we marched to BUS, picking up our guides at LE TRANSLOY. Separate camp is allotted to T.M. Batty. 5 Nisson huts in the camp.	LENS 11 [illegible]
	22nd		Live firing in morning. Experiments with anti-aircraft fire. It was found that there were several ~~objections~~ objections to firing at aeroplanes. Afterwards we experimented with shrapnel fire and ordinary barrage work. Very successful results and very interesting morning. The afternoon time was taken up in cleaning the "duds" and cleaning the guns.	
	23rd		Being Sunday was a light day. PT and lectures in the morning. Rest of the day off.	
	24th		In morning PT followed by drill for the two classes. NCOs had lectures on Prismatic Compass. Night march by compass for NCOs postponed owing to the night being too light.	
	[illegible]		In evening match was arranged between a team of the RBs and a composite team of Brigade HQ, MGC & 17th L.T.M.B. We gave them a good game. Result 2-1 in our favour.	

F. E. Barnwell 2Lt

D. D. & L., London, E.C. (A7883) Wt W809/M1672 750,000 4/17 Sch 52a Forms/C/2118/14

Army Form C. 2118.

Instructions regarding War Diaries and Intelligence Summaries are contained in F. S. Regs., Part II. and the Staff Manual respectively. Title pages will be prepared in manuscript.

WAR DIARY
or
~~INTELLIGENCE SUMMARY.~~
(Erase heading not required.)

Place	Date	Hour	Summary of Events and Information	Remarks and references to Appendices
	25th		From 9 AM – 10.30 AM a PT & BF demonstration under CSM Stokes (AGS). Followed by whole Battery less NCOs doing squad drill: NCOs did the compass march set for them for the previous night. Result good. Afternoon – lecture.	
	26th		P.T. Gun drill for the classes. Practice bomb throwing for remainder of battery. Afternoon – Div baths at Ytres. Advance party went to take over camp at Haut-~~Allines~~ HAUT-ALLAINES.	
HAUT-ALLINES C 29 b 2.4 Sheet 62c	27th		Battery moved to new area at Haut-Allaines in morning. Voluntary bathing in afternoon.	
	28th		PT and squad drill in morning. Cleaning-up parade in afternoon. Advance party left for new camp in Bernes area.	
BERNES – MONTIGNY Fm K 35 b 5.7	29th		Battery moved to new camp at Montigny Fm in Bernes area. A very good camp with good football ground.	
Sheet 62c	30th		Sunday. PT & BF from 9 AM – 10 AM. From 10.30 – 11.30 AM Gun drill for class. Arm drill & squad drill for remainder of battery. 11.45 – 12.30 AM. Gun drill for all. Inspection of tents by battery commander at 10.30 AM. Remainder of the day off.	

F E Barnwell 2Lt

D. D. & L., London, E.C. (A7883) Wt W809/M1672 350,000 4/17 Sch. 52a Forms/C/2118/14

Confidential

War Diary

14th Light Trench Mortar Battery

Vol. 4 October 1917

H F Layton Capt

O.C. 14th L.T.M.B.

17th L.T.M.B.

Army Form C. 2118.

Instructions regarding War Diaries and Intelligence Summaries are contained in F. S. Regs., Part II, and the Staff Manual respectively. Title pages will be prepared in manuscript.

WAR DIARY
or
~~INTELLIGENCE~~ SUMMARY.
(Erase heading not required.)

Place	Date	Hour	Summary of Events and Information	Remarks and references to Appendices
Sheet 62c N.E. Montigny Farm K35 B50.70	1917 Oct. 1st		Battery resting. Two Officers & N.C.Os of Battery reconnoitred the line for gun positions and Trench Mortar Ammunition [illegible] were found.	
	2nd to 6th	Inclusive	Battery supplied working parties for R.E.	
"	7th		Two officers reconnoitred Brown Line with a view of placing guns in position to cover the wire between British and French sectors. It was afterwards decided that these guns would not be required. Remainder of Battery on working parties.	
do	8th, 9th, 10th		Battery still employed on R.E. work. The work was the construction of water horse lines for Brigade at BERNES and also the construction of huts.	
"	11th to 23rd	Inclusive	2 Officers and 18 O.R. were employed in constructing two emplacements for defensive guns in DRAGOON POST. These guns were placed respectively at G31 C40.60 and G31 C70.30 (Sheet 62c N.W.) The remainder of battery carried out the usual [illegible]	

H.W. Layton Capt

D. D. & L., London, E.C.
(A7883) Wt W809/M1672 350,000 4/17 Sch 52a Forms/C/2118/14

19th L.T.M.B.

Army Form C. 2118.

Instructions regarding War Diaries and Intelligence Summaries are contained in F. S. Regs., Part II. and the Staff Manual respectively. Title pages will be prepared in manuscript.

WAR DIARY
or
~~INTELLIGENCE SUMMARY.~~

(Erase heading not required.)

Place	Date	Hour	Summary of Events and Information	Remarks and references to Appendices
Montigny Farm	1917 Oct. 1st – 16th		Training which consisted of P.T. & B.F., Squad and Gun Drill, Gun	
K.35.B.50.70.	23rd		Drill and firing with Dummy ammunition. On the very cold	
Sheet 62c N.E.			mornings, a short cross country run (about 1½ to 2 miles) was	
			held in place of P.T.	
	24th		The gun positions having been completed 1 Officer and 8 O.R.	
			proceeded to the line to man the guns. These guns were	
			not registered as they were for purely defensive purposes	
			and it was considered inadvisable to give the position away.	
	24th – 26th		Remainder of battery carried out usual training. Baths were	
	27th		arranged for the men who had come down from the line.	
	28th		1 Officer and [illegible] other ranks of battery available	
	31st		(30) have been attached to R.E.s, constructing dug-outs	
			and [illegible] trenches in ASCENSION POST (62c N.E. [illegible])	
			No casualties have occurred during month.	
			Total strength of battery (including attached) 5 Offrs 89 O.R.	

J H Layton Capt.

D. D. & L., London, E.C.
(A7883) Wt. W809/M1672 350,000 4/17 Sch. 52a Forms/C/2118/14

Confidential

War Diary

of

17[a] Light Trench Mortar Battery

for

November 1917.

Volume 5

H. F. Layton Capt

O.C. 17[a] L.T.M.B.

Instructions regarding War Diaries and Intelligence Summaries are contained in F. S. Regs., Part II. and the Staff Manual respectively. Title pages will be prepared in manuscript.

WAR DIARY
or
~~INTELLIGENCE SUMMARY.~~
(Erase heading not required.)

Army Form C. 2118.

Place	Date	Hour	Summary of Events and Information	Remarks and references to Appendices
Montigny Farm. Sheet 62 NE K 35 B 8.7	Nov 1-11		1 Officer and 8 men of battery at Dragoon Post with 2 guns in defensive positions. Remainder of battery employed by 104th Coy R.E. building dug-outs etc.	
	11		Headquarters of battery moved to Bernes Q 10 A 10.80 Sheet 62 C S.E.	
Bernes 62 C SE Q 10 a 10.80	15		Battery Commander attended conference at H.Qrs of 72nd Inf Bde with reference to assisting a raid by the 9th East Surreys.	See Appendix II 72 I.B.
— " —	16		Battery Commander reconnoitred left Batt. front of 72nd I.B. for gun positions.	O.O. No 192
— " —	17		1 Off and 16 O.R. proceeded to 72nd I.B. front and placed four guns in position in POND TRENCH (Sheet 62 N.W. F 1 d 40.60)	
— " —	19th		Registration of guns carried out successfully.	
— " —	20th		Zero 6.10 am. Raid by 9th East Surreys. Four guns firing on various points with a view to preventing enemy machine guns from opening fire. This was done successfully, no machine guns firing during the operation. A total of 785 rounds was fired. About midday our four guns were withdrawn and officers and men returned to Head Quarters at Bernes. No casualties.	

D. D. & L., London, E.C.
(A7833) Wt. W803/M1672 350,000 4/17 Sch. 52a Forms C/2118/14

Instructions regarding War Diaries and Intelligence Summaries are contained in F. S. Regs., Part II. and the Staff Manual respectively. Title pages will be prepared in manuscript.

Army Form C. 2118.

WAR DIARY or INTELLIGENCE SUMMARY.

(Erase heading not required.)

Place	Date	Hour	Summary of Events and Information	Remarks and references to Appendices
[illegible] 62c SE	Nov.			
Q.15.a.10.80	20		Working party for R.E. resumed work. Men in DRAGOON POST were relieved by a party from BERNES.	
	21 to 30		Normal routine followed viz 1 Off. + 8 O.R. with two guns at DRAGOON POST and 6 N.C.Os and 32 O.R. at work for R.E.s. Owing to all the men being in the line it has been impossible to carry out any kind of training.	
			Two Military Medals were awarded to N.C.Os of the battery for the part they played in assisting the raid of the East Surreys.	
			Average strength of Battery during month 3 Offs. 54 O.R.	
			Casualties during month – Nil –	

D. D. & L., London, E.C. (A7833) Wt. W593/M1672 350,000 4/17 Sch. 52a Forms/C/2118/14

Not to be taken past Bn. Hd Qrs.

H. W. Layton Capt. COPY NO *6*

72nd INFANTRY BRIGADE OPERATION ORDER NO 192.

16TH November 1917.

Ref. Map.
Corps Top. Sect
T.(9) 2.11.17.

1. Two raids will be carried out on 72nd Infantry Brigade Front on the morning of th[illegible] by :-
(a) 8th The Queens (R.W.S.) Regt. on enemy trenches between G.14.a.2.9. and RAILWAY CUTTING G.8.c.2.3.
(b) 9th East Surrey Regt. on enemy trenches between G.1.d.90.00 and G.2.c.23.57.
for the purpose of inflicting casualties on the enemy, capturing prisoners, and obtaining identifications.

2. Detailed orders have been drawn up by O's.C. Battalions concerned.

3. Both raiding parties will enter the enemy trenches at Zero plus 30 secs. Zero hour will be notified later.

4. O.C. 103rd Field Coy. R.E. will arrange with O.C. 8th The Queens (R.W.S.) Regt and O.C. 9th East Surrey Regt. for R.E. to assist with Bangalore Torpedoes and mobile charges.

5. The 73rd Infantry Brigade are making a raid on enemy trenches between G.1.b.80.40. to G.1.b.95.70. on the same date.
This raiding party will enter the enemy's trenches at Zero plus 5 minutes.

6. Raiding party (s) will be assisted by :-
(1) Artillery as per attached Table.
(2) 4 - 6" Newtons " "
(3) 6 - 3" Stokes

Zero - Zero plus 30 Secs. intensive fire on raid objectives
Zero plus 30 sec. - Zero plus 40 secs.) Firing duds.
Zero plus 1 min. - Zero plus 11 mins.) Lifting to BANK TRENCH.
8 rounds a gun per min. with 2 guns remaining on junction of BANK TRENCH and HIDDEN HAND TRENCH (G.8.c.3.7.)
Zero plus 11 mins - Zero Plus 20 mins.) 4 rounds a gun a min.
Zero plus 20 - Zero plus 30 min.) 6 rounds a gun a min. then cease fire if raiders have withdrawn

(4) 11 M.G's will fire as follows :-
1 gun 72nd Machine Gun Coy. from TURNIP LANE on junction of PAN LANE and Front Line.
2 guns 72nd Machine Gun Coy. enfilade between QUARRIES
2 guns 17th Machine Gun Coy. continue this barrage W. to enemy front line.
4 guns 72nd Machine Gun Coy. Eastern Edge of QUARRY WOOD
2 guns 191st Machine Gun Coy. Northern edge of QUARRY WOOD
All above guns to open fire at Zero and fire for half an hour.

(5) 1 H.T.M. on PIMPLE. G.14.[illegible]

The raiding party (b) will be assisted as follows :-

(1) 4 - 6" Newtons as per attached Table

(2) 4 - 3" Stokes, firing on :-

(a) G.8.a.05.30.

(b) G.7.b.90.90.

(c) G.2.c.25.65.

(d) laid on G.2.c.0.2. in case M.G. opens from here before raiding party enters - then fire on point selected by O.C. 9th East Surrey Regt. and O.C. 72nd Trench Mortar Battery.

Rate of fire as follows :-

0 - 10 mins.	8	rounds	a	gun	per	minute.
10 - 20 "	4	"	"	"	"	"
20 - 30 "	6	"	"	"	"	"

(3) 12 Machine Guns as follows :-

2 guns 72nd Machine Gun Coy. BUCKSHOT RAVINE

4 guns191st Machine Gun Coy. DOE TRENCH, QUENNEMONT TRENCH

2 guns191st Machine Gun Coy. SKIN TRENCH G.8.a.5.9. - G.8.a.6.6.

4 guns191st Machine Gun Coy. Enfilade ROPE LANE from the Junction with SKIN TRENCH

(4) 2 H.T.M's. as per attached Table.

8. Coloured Lights will be put up by 9th East Surrey Regt between G.7.b.7.1. - G.7.b.7.5. where the wire has been cut to confuse the enemy and attract his attention to this point. These lights will not be sent up before Zero plus 30 secs.

9. The signal for the withdrawal will be arranged by Battalions concerned

10. Advanced Battalion H.Q. will be :-

(a) 8th The Queens (R.W.S.) Regt. CART SUPPORT.

(b) 9th East Surrey Regt. POND SUPPORT.

These H.Q. will be in Signal Communication with Brigade Headquarters.

11. Prisoners will be sent via. Battalion H.Q. to Brigade Headquarters, HERVILLY.

12. Watches will be synchronised at 3-0 p.m. and 7.0 p.m. on 19th November at :-

(a) Brigade Headquarters. HERVILLY

(b) THE EGG.

Units concerned will arrange for a representative to attend at one of the above places at times stated.

O.C. 72nd Infantry Brigade Signals will arrange to send a watch to (a) and (b) at times stated

13 Acknowledge.

T. B. Hawley Captain.
Brigade Major.
72nd Infantry Brigade.

COPIES TO :-

1. B.G.C.
2. 24th Division "G".
3. 17th Infantry Brigade.
4. 73rd Infantry Brigade.
5. 17th Machine Gun Company.
6. 17th Trench Mortar Battery.
7. 8th The Queens (R.W.S.) Regt.
8. 9th East Surrey Regt.
9. 8th Royal West Kent Regt.
10. 1st North Staffordshire Regt.
11. 72nd Machine Gun Company.
12. 72nd Trench Mortar Battery.
13. C.R.A.
14. Left Group R.A.
15. D.T.M.O.
16. 191st Machine Gun Company.
17. 103rd Field Coy. R.E.
18. Staff Captain.
19. WAR DIARY.
20. FILE.
21. Signals. 72nd Infantry Brigade.

PROGRAMME OF ARTILLERY SUPPORT FOR RAID "A".

Time	Guns	Objective	Rate of fire
to plus 2 hrs.	6-18-pdrs C/106	FARM TRENCH G.13.b. 98.60.-G.14.a.26.06	0-10' 4 rds a gun a min. 10'-30' 3 rds a gun a min. 30'-1hr. 3rds a gun every 2 mins.
ditto	6-18-pdrs A/107	PAN LANE G.13.b. 98.60.-G.14.a.55.90	1 hr.-2 hrs. 2 rds a gun every 3 mins.
ditto	4-18-pdrs B/106	W. edge of QUARRY WOOD and of NORTHERN QUARRY. G.8.c. 64.26.-G.14.a.7.6.	During period 30'-2hrs., in addition to the above steady rates, bursts of 2 rds gun fire will be fired every five minutes
to plus 2 hrs	~~xx~~6"H.T.M.	High ground(PIMPLE) about G.14.a.3.2.	20 rounds.
to plus 2 hours	1-6"Newton T.Ms.	Trench Junction G.8.c.62.28	0-30' 3 rds a T.M. a min. 30'-1hr. 1 rd a T.M. a min. 1 hr.-2hrs 2 rds a T.M. every 3 mins
ditto	1-6"Newton T.M.	Trench Junction G.14.a.64.84.	
ditto	1-6"Newton T.M.	Point in trench G.8.c.5.1.	
	1 ditto	G.8.c.7.5.	
0 to plus 2 hrs.	2-4.5" Hows. D/106	High ground(PIMPLE) about G.14.a.3.2.	0-10' 3 rds. a How. a min. 10'-30' 2rds a How. a min. 30'-1hr 1 rd a How. a min 1hr.-2hrs. 2 rds a How. every 3 mins.
ditto	2-4.5"Hows. D/106	SOUTHERN QUARRY G.14. Central	

At <u>plus 2 hours</u> 18 - pdrs., 4.5" Hows. and 6" Newton T.Ms. will fire <u>"very slow"</u> (1 round every 4 minutes) till stopped by Left Group Commander. The 9.45" (Long) H.T.M. will cease firing at <u>plus 2 hours.</u>

PROGRAMME OF ARTILLERY SUPPORT FOR RAID "B"

Time	Guns	Objective	Rate of fire
0 to plus 2 hrs.	1 H.T.M.	MACHINE GUN G.9.a.32.68.	20 rounds each
	1 H.T.M.	M.Gs. and Battn H.Q. about G.9.a.56.14	
0 to plus 2 hrs	1-6" Newton T.M.	SKIN TRENCH JUNCTION G.8.a. 60.62.	0-30' 3 rds a T.M. a min. 30'-1hr. 1 rd a T.M. a min. 1 hr.-2hrs. 2 rds a T.M. every 3 mins.
	2-6" Newtons T.M.	M.G. and dugouts G.2.c.7.1.	
	1-6" Newton T.M.	Trench Junction G.7.b.90.60	

To all recipients of 72nd Inf. Bde O.O.192.

O.O. 192/3.

S E C R E T.

AMENDMENT & ADDENDUM
T O
72ND INFANTRY BRIGADE OPERATION ORDER No.192.

---

1. O.C., 8th Bn. The Queen's will arrange to place dummy figures in "NO MAN'S LAND", in vicinity of HETTY and IVY Posts on Y/Z night. He will also arrange to operate these figures from 'ZERO', until they cease to draw fire: in any case stopping at 'ZERO' plus 1 hour.

2. Reference para. 12 of Operation Order No. 192., cancel 7.0 p.m. and substitute 8.30 p.m.

3. If telephonic communication with Brigade is broken, Visual as arranged by the Brigade Signalling Officer, will be used: should weather be too foggy for this, messages will be sent by Runner to Support Battalion H.Q. (COTE WOOD), from whence they will be forwarded to Brigade Headquarters by Fullerphone.

If telephonic communication between Support Battalion Headquarters and Brigade Headquarters is broken, these messages will be sent by runner from Support Battalion Headquarters to Brigade O.P. at L.9.d.05.05., where the B.G.C. will be.

O.C., Support Battalion, will see that his runners are acquainted with this O.P.

T.B. Hankey.
Captain,
Brigade Major, 72nd Infantry Brigade.

18th November, 1917.

CONFIDENTIAL

War Diary

of

17th Light Trench Mortar Battery

for the month of December 1917.

Volume V

H J Layton Capt

O.C. 17th L.T.M.B.

Instructions regarding War Diaries and Intelligence Summaries are contained in F. S. Regs., Part II. and the Staff Manual respectively. Title pages will be prepared in manuscript.

WAR DIARY

or

~~INTELLIGENCE SUMMARY.~~

(*Erase heading not required.*)

Army Form C. 2118.

Volume 5.

Place	Date	Hour	Summary of Events and Information	Remarks and references to Appendices
BERNES 62C NE	DEC: 1st 1.12.17		N.C.O's and men of Battery attached to R.E. for the Construction of Dug-outs in ASCENSION	
			POSTS (MAP REF. 62B N.W. G31b) were relieved and returned to BERNES.	
	2nd 12		During the day twenty men of the Battery were employed in moving S.A.A., Bombs +	
LE VERGUIER 62B N.W. L33a			GRENADES from Cellar rear of LE VERGUIER to the 12th Brigade Bomb Store	
			Lists forwarded to Brigade	
	3rd 12		Battery less two teams carried out Parades. Physical Drill, Arm Drill, Gun Drill	
DRAGOON POST 62B N.W. G31a.90.50	3rd 12 – 4th 12		Two teams relieved from DRAGOON POST by our own men	
	5th 12		Battery carried out Training according to Programme	
			O.C. Battery called to 12th Brigade H.Q. re co-operation with Infantry in Raid	
			Four Guns with teams sent up to 12th Brigade Front in readiness for following	
			day	
	6th 12		Two officers of Battery to 12th Brigade positions. Guns not required. Four teams	
			with Guns returned to BERNES	
HANCOURT 62C [illegible]	7th 12		Two teams relieved from DRAGOON POST. Battery moved to HANCOURT	

D. D. & L., London, E.C.
(A7853) Wt. W809/M1672 350,000 4/17 Sch. 52a Forms C/2118/14

Instructions regarding War Diaries and Intelligence Summaries are contained in F. S. Regs., Part II. and the Staff Manual respectively. Title pages will be prepared in manuscript.

WAR DIARY
or
~~INTELLIGENCE SUMMARY.~~
(*Erase heading not required.*)

Army Form C. 2118.

Place	Date	Hour	Summary of Events and Information	Remarks and references to Appendices
	DEC. 8th 12th to 17th 12.		During this period the Battery carried out Training according to Programme. Gun Drill, Physical Drill, Arm & Infantry Drill, Firing Dummy & Live Shells, Musketry.	
TEMPLEUX LE GERARD 62 C NE L23 b 90.10	18th 12		Battery moved to TEMPLEUX LE GERARD in accordance with 17th I.B. O.O. No 210. Two Officers & Six Gun Teams relieved 73rd Brigade L.T.M.B in the line.	Index No. 1
HARGICOURT D.G. POSITIONS 62 C NE L4 c 90.50	19th 12		Guns Registered. Situation quiet generally. Remainder of Battery engaged on positions in HARGICOURT (Defensive Gun Positions) in accordance with G2/72.	Index No. 2
	20th 12		From the line nothing to report. Remainder of Battery on Defensive G.P.	
	21st 12		From the line. Enemy Minenwerfer activity, shells in and on RUBY TRENCH G.15.10.30. No Casualties. Remainder of Battery on Defensive G.P.	
	22nd 12 to 24th 12		Nothing of importance to report from the line. Our Defensive Positions finished.	
	25th 12		From the line. Enemy Minenwerfer Shells on RUBY TRENCH G.15.10.30. exploding Shell (STOKES 3") Dump. No Casualties.	
	26th 12		Nothing to Report.	
	27th 12		Six Gun Teams in the line relieved by the Remainder of Battery.	

D. D. & L., London, E.C.
(A7883) Wt. W803/M1672 350,000 4/17 Sch. 52a Forms/C/2118/14

Instructions regarding War Diaries and Intelligence Summaries are contained in F. S. Regs., Part II, and the Staff Manual respectively. Title pages will be prepared in manuscript.

WAR DIARY
or
~~INTELLIGENCE SUMMARY.~~
(Erase heading not required.)

Army Form C. 2118.

Place	Date	Hour	Summary of Events and Information	Remarks and references to Appendices
TEMPLEUX-LE-GERARD	DEC.			
62C N° L28 a 90.10	28th 12		From the line nothing to report. Remainder of Battery on Defensive Gun Positions	
	29th 12		" " " Slight activity of enemy artillery. One casualty by shrapnel (slightly wounded)	
			Remainder of Battery on Defensive G.P.s	
	30th 12		From the line nothing to report. Defensive G.P. No 2 finished	
	31st 12			
			Casualties 2. Wounded	
			Battery Strength Officers O.R.	
			4 46	
			H. J. Layton Capt.	
			OC 17th Brigade L.T.M.B.	
			December 31st 1917.	

D. D. & L., London, E.C. (A7883) Wt. W5o3/M1672 350,000 3/17 Sch. 52a Forms/C/2118/14

SECRET G.2/72

8th Buffs
1st Royal Fusiliers
12th Royal Fusiliers
3rd Rifle Brigade
17th M.G.Coy
17th L.T.M.Btty
12th Sherwood Foresters
180th Tunnelling Coy R.E.
129th Field Coy R.E.
10th M.G.Squadron
24th Division "G"(For information)

B.G.C.
Bde Major
Staff Captain
Sigs.17th I.Bde

1. Attached Table shews Battle Positions to be occupied by Supports. Reserves and Details in the Brigade Area in the event of Alarm.

2. C.O's will ensure that the positions, as affecting them, and the approaches thereto are carefully reconnoitred forthwith.

3. A Certificate that this Order has been complied with will be rendered to these Headquarters.

4. ACKNOWLEDGE.

20/12/17

W.A. Mackenzie
Captain.
Brigade Major 17th Infy. Bde.

Table shewing "BATTLE POSITIONS" to be occupied by Supports. Reserves and Details in Brigade Area in event of Alarm or on receipt of Code Word "HOT" from Bde H.Qrs

Serial No	Unit.	Strength	Normal Position	Battle Position Garrison	Battle Position Position	Remarks
1.	Suggested Battle Positions RIGHT BATTALION	--				
	Support Company.	2 Platoons 1 Platoon	POND Support LEICESTER LOUNGE	2 Platoons 1 "	POND Support SLAG TRENCH L.11.b.9.8	 Strong Point to be constructed
	Reserve Coy	1 Company	LEICESTER LOUNGE	2 Platoons 1 Platoon	SLAG TRENCH L.6.c.1.1 BOBBY FARM	Strong Point to be constructed. " "
	Remaining Coy	1 Company	L.10.a.	1 Company	COTE TRENCH from Lt.Railway to L.10.d.3.8	Under Command of Reserve Battalion.
2.	CENTRE BATTALION Support Company.	3 Platoons.	COLOGNE RESERVE	1½ Platoons 1½ "	L.6.c.8.5)COLOGNE L.6.c.6.8)RESERVE.	
	Reserve Company (From Res.Bn).	3 Platoons	QUARRY L.5.b.4.3	1 Platoon 1 Platoon 1 Platoon	L.5.b.45.37) L.5.d.3.8) L.5.d.3.5)	Under orders of Centre Battalion.
	Battalion H.Q		L.5.b.3.2		L.5.b.3.1	

Serial No.	Unit.	Strength.	Normal Position.	Battle Position Garrison	Battle Position Position.	Remarks
3.	LEFT BATTALION Support Company.	1 Platoon 1 Platoon 1 Platoon	ARTAXERXES POST VALLEY POST HUSSAR POST	1 Platoon. 1 " 1 "	ARTAXERXES POST VALLEY POST HUSSAR POST	
	Reserve Company	2 Platoons 1 Platoon	HUSSAR RD NORTH " " SOUTH	2 " 1 "	BENJAMIN SWITCH(F.23.a & c) BENJAMIN SWITCH) (near ARTAXERXES POST)	
	Remaining Coy.	1 Platoon 1 Platoon 1 Platoon	TOINE POST ORCHARD POST HARDY BANKS	1 " 1 " 1 "	HILL POST ORCHARD POST TOINE POST	When mined accommodation is completed in vicinity of HILL POST.-the normal position and Battle Position of each platoon would remain the same viz :- 1 platoon HILL POST 1 " TOINE POST 1 " ORCHARD POST.
	Battalion H.Q		F.28.a.4.7		TOINE TRENCH	
4.	RESERVE BATTN.	2 Companies (less 1 Platoon).	TEMPLEUX QUARRIES	2 Companies (less 1 platoon).	TEMPLEUX QUARRIES	Mobile Reserve under orders of B.G.C and under Command of C.O
		1 Platoon	do	1 Platoon	Garrison for M.G's in TEMPLEUX SWITCH	- -
		1 Company	L.10.a.	1 Company	HARGICOURT Trench North.of TEMPLEUX-HARGICOURT Road.as detailed in (1)	Under Command of 2nd in Command.
		1 Company	QUARRY L.5.b.4.3			Under orders of O.C. Centre Battalion.
5.	12th Sherwood Foresters	4 Companies	TEMPLEUX QUARRIES	4 Companies(less 2 platoons). 2 platoons	SHERWOOD TRENCH CONNOR POST (F.28.d.4.4)	 (Not yet completed)

Serial No.	Unit.	Strength.	Normal Position.	Garrison	Battle Position Position	Remarks
6.	Attached Infantry 180th Tun.Coy R.E	80 O.R.	SLAG HEAP CAMP L.3.c.9.8	40 O.R.	HARGICOURT Tr. N. of TEMPLEUX-HARGICOURT Rd.	Officer i/c to report in HARGICOURT Trench to 2nd in Command Reserve Battalion for orders.
				40 O.R.	HARGICOURT Tr between TEMPLEUX-HARGICOURT Rd and Lt.Rly.	
7.	Details T.M's		HARGICOURT		L.5.a.cent.(approx).	Position not yet constructed. To act as garrison for proposed M.G.Emplacement.
8.	Bde M.G.Coy	2 Reserve guns	TEMPLEUX L.2.b.9.1	1 Reserve Gun 1 " "	L.3.c.04.14 L.3.c.58.87.	Details will act as garrison to M.G's
9.	10th M.G. Squadron	4 Officers 8 Guns(1 N.C.O & 6 men each).	"A" Post F.28.b.7.3. "B" Post F.28.a.1.1 "C" " F.27.d.1.8 "D" " F.27.a.8.7 "E" " F.26.b.5.5 "G" " F.26.b.1.9 "H" " F.20.c.8.1 "K" " F.19.d.4.7			In Left Flank defences. In case of attack to be reinforced by Infantry and 5 L.Guns.
		H.Qrs at "F" Post.				
10.	Bde T M.Btty	Reserve guns & details.	TEMPLEUX L.2.b.9.1	2 Reserve guns	HARGICOURT Trench N. & S. of TEMPLEUX -HARGICOURT Rd.	Under orders of B.G.C. Positions and Ammn. Dump to be prepared.
11.	Det.129th Field Coy R.E	2 Sections & Attd.Infy.	TEMPLEUX L.2.d.1.8	2 sections & Attd.Infy.	Strong point in vicinity of billets.	

SECRET

Copy No ...9...

17th INFANTRY BRIGADE OPERATION ORDER No 210

Ref Map 1/40,000
Sheet 62.c. &
Trench Map

1.(a) The 17th Infy. Bde will relieve the 73rd Infy Bde in the Left Bde Sector of the 24th Div. on the 19/20th Decr and on the 21st Decr. will take over the Left Coy Front of the 72nd Infy Bde.

(b) The relief will be carried out in accordance with Table "A" attached

2. The 17th Infy Bde Front will then be divided into Three Sub-sectors:

RIGHT)
CENTRE) Subsectors, each held by 1 Battalion
Left)

The 4th Battalion less 1 Coy) will be in Bde Reserve with 1 Coy in Reserve to the Centre Sub sector (vide Map Attached, to Bns only).

3. Boundaries will be as under :-

SOUTHERN BOUNDARY

L.7.b.5.7.-CLUB TRENCH (inclusive) to 2nd Dis. Cav. Division-L.11.b.6.5-The EGG (inclusive) to 2nd Dis. Cav. Div.-L.11.c.1.8.-L.10.c.1.9-COTE WOOD H.Qrs inclusive to 2nd Dis. Cav. Div.

BETWEEN RIGHT & CENTRE SUBSECTOR

G.1.d.7.4 (FISH LANE-ONIOW LANE inclusive to Right Battalion)-L.6.c.5.2.-thence along track to L.6.c.10.55-Fork Roads L.5.c.20.35.

BETWEEN CENTRE & LEFT SUBSECTOR

F.30.c.3.7. (CARBINE TRENCH inclusive to Centre Bn)-Cross Rds F.29.d.80.15-thence along track to Rd junction L.5.b.25.70-L.5.a.65.55.

NORTHERN BOUNDARY

A.19.b.00.00-F.23.central-F.22.central-thence track through F.22.c.- F.21.d.-F.27 to Cemetery F.26.d.7.2.

4. One man per Vickers Gun will be left behind for 24 Hours after the relief of thr Gun has taken place.

5. All Guns of the 73rd L.T.M. Battery will be taken over. O.C. 17th L.T.M. Battery will arrange to hand over all his Guns to O.C 73rd L.T.M. Battery.

6a In all cases 1 Guide per Platoon and 1 for Bn H.Qrs will be provided. An Officer is being sent to each separate Rendezvous to co-ordinate guides.

7. All Trench Stores, Trench Maps, Aeroplane Photos. Defence Scheme, Schemes of work in hand and proposed, will be taken over. Receipts for above will be forwarded to Bde H.Qrs as soon as possible after relief.

8. All other details will be arranged direct between C.O's concerned.

9. Completion of relief will be reported to Bde H.Q. by Code Word ....WINDY.

10. B.G.C. 17th Infy. Bde will take over Command of the Left Sector (73rd I.Bde Front) at 10 a.m. on 20th inst. and of the portion of 72nd I.Bde front at 9-30 a.m. on 21st inst.

(Contd).

11. Bde.H.Qrs will be established at HAUTE WOOD at 10 a.m. on Dec 20th at which hour all Units in 73rd I.Bde sector not mentioned in this order will come under the order of the B.G.C 17th I.Bde.

12. ACKNOWLEDGE

Issued to Sigs at
9 p.m.
16/12/17

D.A. Mackenzie
Captain.
Brigade Major 17th Infantry Bde.

Copy No		Copy No	
1	B.G.C.	2	Bde Major
3	Staff Captain	4	8th Buffs
5	1st Roy. Fus	6	12th Roy. Fus
7	3rd R.Bde	8	17th M.G.Coy
9	17th L.T.M.Btty	10	B.T.O.
11	B.S.O.	12	72nd I.Bde
13	73rd I.Bde	14	47th I.Bde
15	"G" 24th Div.	16	"Q" 24th Div.
17	2nd Dis. Cav. Div.	18	24th D.A.
19	Left Group	20	C.R.E.
21	104th Coy R.E.	22	129 Coy RE.
23	D.M.G.O.	24	24th Div. Train.
25	S.S.SO.	26	A.D.M.S.
27	73rd F.A.	28	74th F.A.
29	A.P.M.	30	Div. Gas. Officer
31	12th Sherwood Fors.	32	180 T.Coy.
33	War Diary	34	File.

Relief Table "A" issued with 17th [illegible] O.O. [illegible]

Date	Unit	From	To	Relieving	Guides Rendezvous	Time	Remarks.
18th Dec.	12th R.Fus:	BERNES.	TEMPLEUX QUARRIES (F.27.c.&L.10.a.)	9th Royal Sussex.	CRUCIFIX. L.3.c.70.75.)	3-30.p.m.	Clear of BERNES by 2.p.m.
"	1st R.Fus:	VENDELLES.	HERVILLY.	7th Northamptonshire Regt.			Clear of VENDELLES by 2-30.p.m.
18/19th Dec.	17th M.G.C.	VRAIGNES.	Line.	73rd M.G.C.	L.2.b.6.4.		(As arranged by C.O's (concerned. Move to (Forward Area by lorry.
	17th L.T.M.B.	HANCOURT.	Line.	73rd L.T.M.B.	---- do ----		
19/20th Dec.	12th R.Fus:	TEMPLEUX QUARRIES & L.10.a.	Centre Sub-sector.	2nd Leinsters. Rt Front Line Cy Left Front Coy.) Support Coy.)	L.10.a. TEMPLEUX QUARRIES.	3.45.p.m. 3.30.p.m.	
				13th Mddx Regt. Rt Front Line Cy.	L.10.a.	--do--	
	3rd R.Bde.	HANCOURT.	Centre Sub-sector.	2nd Leinsters. (Reserve Coy).	TEMPLEUX QUARRIES.	--do--	Under orders of O.C. 12th Royal Fusiliers.
	1st R.Fus:	HERVILLY.	Left Sub-sector.	13th Mddx. (3 Coys).	Left Bn H.Q. F.28.a.4.7.		1. As arranged between C.O's concerned. 2. Remaining Coy will be accommodated at HARDY BANKS and ORCHARD POST.
20th Dec.	3rd R.Bde. (3 Coys).	HANCOURT.	TEMPLEUX QUARRIES (2 Coys). L.10.a. (1 Coy).	2nd Leinsters. (3 Coys).	CRUCIFIX. (L.3.c.70.75.)	3-30.p.m.	
21st Dec.	8th Buffs.	BERNES & MONTIGNY FARM.	Left Sub-sector.	8th R.W.Kents. (3 Coys).	CRUCIFIX. (L.3.c.70.75.)	10.a.m.	1. 1 Coy at L.10.a. accommodation vacated by 1 Coy 2nd Leinsters.

BATTALION HEADQUARTERS at LEICESTER LOUNGE L.11.b.4.7.

NOTE. All movement E.of HERVILLY will be by platoons at 200 yards interval.

Confidential

War Diary

of

14th Light Trench Mortar Battery

for month of January 1918.

Volume VI.

H. G. Layton Capt

O.C. 14th L.T.M.B.

Instructions regarding War Diaries and Intelligence Summaries are contained in F. S. Regs., Part II. and the Staff Manual respectively. Title pages will be prepared in manuscript.

WAR DIARY or ~~INTELLIGENCE SUMMARY.~~

(Erase heading not required.)

Army Form C. 2118.

Volume VI

Place	Date	Hour	Summary of Events and Information	Remarks and references to Appendices
	JAN. 1918 1st to 5th		During this time the Battery were in the line, Nothing of importance to Report.	
HERVILLY Map 62C K23d 80.60	5th/6th		The Battery was relieved by the 73RD L.T.M.B. & proceeded to HERVILLY	
	6th to 13th		The Battery while at HERVILLY carried out work for the defense of their Hutments and when possible carried on with their usual Training.	
TEMPLEUX. Map Ref HARGICOURT Special Sheet L 26 90.05	13th/14th		Battery proceeded to TEMPLEUX where they relieved the 72nd L.T.M.B, one section took over positions in the line.	B.O.O. 215
			O.C. Battery reconnoitred "Intermediate Area" for positions of Guns in the defense of the "Intermediate Line" positions & map references forwarded to 17th Brigade	
HUSSAR POST. Map Ref HARGICOURT Special Sheet L29b 50.15	15th		3inch Stokes Ammunition, reported dumped in the vicinity of HUSSAR POST. an officer located same & reported on its condition	
Map Ref HARGICOURT S.m HARGICOURT. L5.c 90.70.	16th		Ammunition (3" Stokes) salved from HUSSAR POST. & taken to SALVAGE DUMP at HARGICOURT.	
	17th		Gun positions found & prepared to take eight Guns to assist in forthcoming Raid by the 3rd Battn The RIFLE BRIGADE, some of these Guns registered.	

D. D. & L., London, E.C. (A7883) Wt. W593/M1672 350,000 4/17 Sch. 52a Forms/C/2118/14

Instructions regarding War Diaries and Intelligence Summaries are contained in F. S. Regs., Part II, and the Staff Manual respectively. Title pages will be prepared in manuscript.

WAR DIARY

or

~~INTELLIGENCE SUMMARY.~~

(Erase heading not required.)

Army Form C. 2118.

Volume VI.

Place	Date	Hour	Summary of Events and Information	Remarks and references to Appendices
	JAN 1918 18th 19th		Remainder of Guns Registered & reported, final preparation of position & ammunition made.	
	20th		The Battery supported the Raid with success.	B.O. 218. Appx II
			The weather conditions during days 15th–20th are noted, after the heavy frost the weather turned warmer & much rain fell, positions had to be redug & in some cases new ones found. During the firing on the 20th the ground was in such a condition as to cause "Base Plates" to sink deep into the earth causing incorrect fire which was corrected repeatedly	
HANCOURT. MAP REF 62C. P.8.b.30.30.	21st		Battery relieved proceeding to HANCOURT by train	B.O.O. 219. Appx III
	22nd		Battery inspection, Guns cleaned.	
	23rd/28th		These days were allotted to Training, "Gun Drill, Arm Drill, Gas Drill, Musketry, Map Reading etc. & the improvement of Camp, new paths being made, Trenches & embankments round each Hut.	
HANCOURT MAP REF 62C. P.3.a.6.	29th		Battery on "Range" at HANCOURT, where they carried out, firing practice with Rifles & Revolvers, firing 3" Stokes Shells on targets & experimental shooting with 3" Stokes Shells.	

[initials]

D. D. & L., London, E.C. (A5833) Wt. W593/M1672 350,000 4/17 Sch. 52a Forms C/2118/14

Army Form C. 2118.

WAR DIARY
or
~~INTELLIGENCE SUMMARY.~~
(Erase heading not required.)

Instructions regarding War Diaries and Intelligence Summaries are contained in F. S. Regs., Part II, and the Staff Manual respectively. Title pages will be prepared in manuscript.

Volume VI

Place	Date	Hour	Summary of Events and Information	Remarks and references to Appendices
HESBECOURT. MAP 62C L 13.C	JAN. 1918 30th		Battery found a working party to assist in making cable pits in front of HESBECOURT. They were out from 8.30 am to 5.30 pm	
	31st		Usual Training programme adhered to, attached men from the 8th BUFFS returned to their unit, men from the QUEENS & 1st R.F. replacing them.	K 105 App. IV K 105.
			Casualties Nil Average Strength Offrs 4 O.R. 52	

D. D. & L., London, E.C. (A7833) Wt. W703/M1672 350,000 1/17 Sch. 52a Forms C/2118/14

Appendix I

S E C R E T

Copy ...10......

17th INFANTRY BRIGADE OPERATION ORDER No 215.

1. The 17th Inf. Bde will relieve the 72nd Inf. Bde in the Line between the 12th and 14th January. Relief to be completed by 6 a.m. 14th January.

2. The relief will be carried out in accordance with Table "A" attached.

3. The following intervals will be maintained on the march :- Between Platoons - 200 yards, and between each 6 Transport vehicles - 200 yards.

4. O.C. 17th L.T.M.Btty will take over the guns of the 72nd L.T.M.Btty in the Line.

5. All other details will be arranged direct by C.O's concerned.

6. All Look-Out Posts and A.A.Vickers Gun and Lewis Gun positions will be handed over.

7. All Defence Schemes, Aeroplane Photographs, Sunprints, Sketches, Trench Stores etc., will be taken over and receipts sent to Brigade H.Qrs as soon as possible after relief.

8. Completion of relief will be wired to Brigade H.Qrs by Code Word ...."TANK".

9. Command of the Sector will pass to B.G.C. 17th I.Bde at 6 p.m. 13th January, at which hour 17th I.Bde H.Qrs will close at BERNES and open at HAUTE WOOD.

10. ACKNOWLEDGE.

Issued to Sigs at 9 pm

....

10/1/18

[signature] Captain.

A/Brigade Major 17th Infantry Bde.

Copy No	To	Copy No	To
1	B.G.C.	2	Bde Major.
3	Staff Captain	4	8th Buffs
5	1st Roy. Fus	6	12th Roya Fus.
7	3rd Rifle Bde	8	17th M.G.Coy
9	Sigs 17th I.Bde	10	17th L.T.M.Battery
11	B.T.O.	12	B.S.O.
13	72nd I.Bde	14	73rd I.Bde
15	"G" 24th Div.	16	"Q" 24th Div.
17	2nd Dis Cav Div.	18	Left Brigade
19	24th D.A.	20	Left Group R.F.A.
21	C.R.E.	22	104th Field Coy R.E.
23	129th Field Coy R.E.	24	D.M.G.O.
25	23th Div. Train	26	S.S.O.
27	A.D.M.S.	28	73rd Field Amb.
29	74th Field Amb.	30	A.P.M.
31	Div. Gas Officer	32	12th Sherwood Fors.
33	258th T.Coy R.E.	34	War Diary
35	File	36	

Table "A" to accompany 17th Infantry Brigade O.O. No. 15

Date	Unit.	From	To	Relieving	Remarks.
Jan 12/13th.	3rd Rifle Bde.	VENDELLES	Centre Sub-Sector.	8th Queens	
"	12th Roy.Fus.	BERNES	Brigade Reserve	1st N.Staffords	Relief to be complete by 3-30 p.m.
"	17th M.G.Coy	HERVILLY MONTIGNY TEMPLEUX SWITCH	Line	72nd M.G.Coy	Details to be arranged by C.O's concerned.
Jan 13/14th	1st Roy. Fus.	HERVILLY	Left Sub-Sector	9th E.Surreys	Details to be arranged by C.O's concerned.
"	8th Buffs	MONTIGNY	Right Sub-Sector	8th R.W.Kents	-do-
"	17th L.T.M.Btty	HERVILLY	Line	72nd L.T.M.Btty	-do-

Appendix II

Copy No ......6.

SECRET

17th INFANTRY BRIGADE OPERATION ORDER No 218

Ref. HARGICOURT Special Sheet

Ed. 1a. 1/10,000

1. A raid on the enemy's trenches in A.25.d. will be carried out on the morning of the 20th.

2. The raid will be carried out by 3rd Rifle Brigade.
The Raiding Party will consist of :-
3 Officers and 46 O.R. 3rd Rifle Bde.
5 O.R. 104th Field Coy R.E.
Area to be raided will be enemy front and support line from A.25.d.30.10 -A.25.d.18.50- A.25.d.30.33.

3. The raiding parties will leave our trenches at MINNOW TRENCH A.25.d.15.00 and MALAKOFF TRENCH F.30.d.95.20.

4. ZERO Hour will be notified later.

5. The raid will be carried out according to separate detailed orders of O.C. 3rd Rifle Bde.(Copies to all Units 17th I.Bde).

6. The following signals will be used :-

(a) For information of actual Raiding Party.

Objectives gained ....2 Green Very Lights (One light by each party).

Withdraw ....1 Red Very Light.

(b) For information of Artillery

All Clear .... 1 Gold and Silver Rain Rocket fired from SUGAR TR(L.6.a.85.85) in direction of HARGICOURT.

7. Artillery. The detailed Artillery Programme is attached as App "A". (To Units 17th I.Bde only).
This programme has been issued by 24th D.A. to all concerned. (except Units 17th I.Bde).

8. 3" Stokes Mortars. At ZERO the 17th L.T.M.Btty will put down Barrage on German Front Line A.25.d.30.10 - 10.32-20.60.
At ZERO plus 3 the 3" Stokes Mortars will lift and form Blocks in trenches at A.25.d.50.05 and A.25.d.20.75(Duds will be fired from Z plus 2' 45" to ZERO plus 3').
The 3" Stokes Mortars will cease fire when the " All Clear"signal is fired.

9. M.G.Programme A detailed programme and map is attached as App "B".

10. The 3" Stokes Mortars and M.G's will take their time from the Artillery and will open fire immediately on the Artillery Barrage being put down at ZERO.

11. Synchronisation of Watches
(a) A special D.R. from 17th I.B. will meet S.D.R. from 24th D.A. at Right Group H.Qrs at 10-30 p.m. on 19th inst for the purpose of synchronising watches.
(b) All Units 17th I.B. will send a representative (with 2 Watches) to report to Bde Signalling Officer at Bde H.Qrs(L.7.c.30.25) at 11 p.m. 19th inst.

(Contd).

12. Medical Arrang ments.
2 Stretched bearers will be in a Dugout in BOWER LANE (L.6.a. 95.95) and 2 Stretched bearers in a dugout in MALAKOFF TR (F.30.c.95.20).
The Advanced Aid Post will be in SUGAR TRENCH(L.6.a.85.85).
Cases will be cleared from HARGICOURT by Motor Ambulance.

13. Inn order to distract the attention of the enemy Two demonstrations will be mado :-
    1. At about G.1.c.60.05 under orders of O.C.8th Buffs.
    2. At about F.30.a.30.95 under orders of O.C.1st Royal Fusiliers.
Dummy figures will be used in these demonstrations covered, if the wind is favourable by smoke clouds and in any case by intense Lewis Gun Fire.

14. All Working Parties in the Brigade Area will be withdrawn 30 minutes before ZERO and no Working Party will be sent out until one hour after ZERO.

Issued to Sigs
at...........
18/1/18

[signature]
Captain.
A/Brigade Major 17th Infantry Bde.

Copy No 1 to 3rd Riflo Bde   Copy No 2 to 8th Buffs

3	12th Roy. Fus.	4	1st Roy. Fus.
5	17th M.G.Coy	6	17th L.T.M.Btty
7	B.G.C. 17th I.B,	8	B.M. 17th I.B.
9	24th Div. "G"	10	24th D.A.
11	104th Fiel Coy R.E.	12	

Appendix III

SECRET

Copy No. 9

17th INFANTRY BRIGADE OPERATION ORDER No 219

Ref. Maps 62.c.1/40,000
HARGICOURT special sheet
Ed. 1.a.1/10,000

1. The 17th Infantry Bde will be relieved in the Line by the 73rd I.Bde on the 20/21st and 21/22nd January 1918.
Reliefs will be complete by 6 a.m. 22nd January.
On relief 17th I.Bde will be Brigade in Corps Reserve.

2. All moves will be in accordance with Table "A" attached.

3. The following intervals will be maintained on the March, between platoons 200 yards and between each 6 Transport vehicles 200 yards.

4. Staff Captain will arrange for representative from Bde H.Qrs to be at entraining point on 20th and 21st inst. This Officer will supervise entraining of all Units. C.O's concerned will send an Officer to reconnoitre entraining Point forthwith.

5. All Trench stores, aeroplane photos, defence schemes, tables of work in hand and proposed, lists of pass words etc., will be handed over and receipts sent to Bde H.Qrs as soon as possible after relief.

6. Details of Look-out Posts, Camp Defences, A.A.Lewis Gun positions and details regarding Bomb proof defences round hutments, in the Reserve area will be taken over.

7. 17th M.G.Coy will take over A.A.positions at HANCOURT DUMP.

8. Light T.M's in the Line will be handed over.

9. Units will notify Bde H.Qrs of completion of relief by wiring time at which relief is completed.

10. All other details will be arranged by C.O's concerned.

11. Command of present 17th I.Bde sector will pass to B.G.C., 73rd I.Bde at 6 p.m. 21st Jan. at which hour the B.G.C. 17th I.Bde will assume Command of Brigade in Corps Reserve and 17th I.Bde Office will close at HAUT WOOD and open at VRAIGNES.

12. ACKNOWLEDGE.

[signature]
Captain.
A/Brigade Major 17th Infantry Bde.

Issued to Sigs at
6 p.m. 18/1/18

Copy No		Copy No	
1	to B.G.C.	2	to Bde Major
3	Staff Captain	4	8th Buffs
5	1st Roy. Fus	6	12th Roy. Fus
7	3rd R.Bde	8	17th M.G.Coy
9	17th L.T.M.Btty	10	Sigs 17th I Bde
11	B.T.O.	12	B.S.O.
13	195 Coy A.S.C.	14	72nd I.Bde
15	73rd I.Bde	16	"G" 24th Div.
17	"Q" 24th Div.	18	2nd Dis Cav Div.
19	Left Infy Bde	20	C.R.A.
21	Left Group R.F.A.	22	C.R.E.
23	104th Field Coy R.E.	24	129th Field Coy
25	D.M.G.O.	26	24th Div. Train
27	S.S.O.	28	A.D.M.S.
29	74th Field Amb.	30	73rd Field Amb.
31	Div. Gas Officer	32	A.P.M.
33	12th Sherwoods	34	258th T.Coy R.E.
35	War Diary	36	File.

Table "A" issued with 17th I.Bde O.O. 219

Serial No.	Date.	Unit	From	To	Route	Relieved by	Remarks
1.	20/1/18	3rd Rifle Bde	Bde Support	VRAIGNES Camp Camp "B"	Route March to ROISEL, thence by Light Railway to VRAIGNES or HANCOURT	9th R.Sussex Rgt.	Entrain ROISEL 6 p.m. at C.Y.205(K'12.a.55.9).
2	-do-	12th R.Fus.	Centre Sector	VRAIGNES		7th Northampton-Shire Rgt.	Entrain at C.Y.205 at 9 p.
3	-do-	17th M.G.C	Line	VRAIGNES		73rd M.G.Coy	Entrain at C.Y 205 at 9 p.
4.	21/1/18	1st R.Fus	Left subsector	HANCOURT (Camp "A")		13th Middlesex	Entrain CY 205 at 6 p.m.
5	-do-	8th Buffs	Right Subsector	HANCOURT		2nd Leinster Rgt	Entrain CY 205 at 8 p.m.
6.	-do-	17th T.M.Btty	Line	HANCOURT		73rd T.M.Btty	Entrain C.Y 205 at 8 p.m.

Appendix IV

SECRET

17th I.Bde
K.105

1. Personnel of the 8th Bn The Buffs and 12th Bn Royal Fusiliers employed away from their Units will be relieved by 6 p.m. on Wednesday Jan 30th according to the following lists :-

A. 8th Bn The Buffs.

Employed at	Numbers Off.	N.C.O's	O.R	To be relieved by	At.
104th Coy R.E.	1	1	23	8th Queens	ROISEL.
17th M.G.Coy			4	-do-	VRAIGNES.
191st M.G.Coy			4	-do-	ROISEL
17th T.M.Btty			5	-do-	HANCOURT
Div.Disbursing Off.			1	-do-	ROISEL
Div. Reinfct.Off Railhead. Clerk			1	-do-	PERONNE.
258th Tun.Coy R.E.		1	42	1st R.Fus.	VRAIGNES.
24th Div Baths & Laundry.			6	3rd R.Bde	ROISEL.
24th Depot Bn.			4	-do-	CURLU.
Area Comdt.			3	-do-	HERVILLY.
12th Sherwood Foresters	1	1	26	-do-	ROISEL.
Water Point, BOUVINCOURT.			1	-do-	BOUVINCOURT
Y.M.C.A., BERNES			1	-do-	BERNES.

B. 12th Bn Royal Fusiliers.

	Off.	N.C.O's	O.R		
104th Coy R.E	1	1	24	1st R.Fus.	ROISEL.
17th M.G.Coy			4	-do-	VRAIGNES.
258th Tun. Coy R.E.			~~4~~	-do-	VRAIGNES.
17th T.M.Btty	1	-	6	-do-	HANCOURT.
Div. Baths.			6	-do-	ROISEL.
Depot Bn.		1(Sgt)		3rd R.Bde	CURLU
A.P.M. for Level Crossings.			3	-do-	HANCOURT Crossing.
Officers' Club.			1	-do-	MONTIGNY
Railhead Disbursing Clerk			1	-do-	ROISEL.
Corps Reinfct Camp.			3	-do-	FLAMICOURT (PERONNE).

2. Units sending these reliefs will forward a written statement with each shewing exactly whom they are to relieve.

3. Units to whom the above details are attached will please arrange to return men of the 8th Buffs and 12th Royal Fusiliers to their Units (at HANCOURT & VRAIGNES respectively) immediately on Relief.

4. ACKNOWLEDGE.

W R G Byrne
Captain.

28/1/18

Staff Captain 17th Infantry Brigade.

Copies to:- 8th Buffs
12th Royal Fus.
8th Queens
17th M.G.Coy
104th Field Coy R.E.
H.Q. 72nd I.Bde (For information).
1st Royal Fus.
3rd R.Bde
12th Sherwood Foresters
17th L.T.M.Btty
258th Tun. Coy R.E.

Confidential

War Diary of the 17th Light Trench Mortar Battery for February 1918.

28/2/1918

W R Jakeman 2/Lt
for Capt Commanding 17th L.T.M.B.

D. D. & L., London, E.C.
(A7833) Wt. W803/M1672 350,000 4/17 Sch. 52a Forms/C/2118/14

Instructions regarding War Diaries and Intelligence Summaries are contained in F. S. Regs., Part II. and the Staff Manual respectively. Title pages will be prepared in manuscript.

WAR DIARY of ~~INTELLIGENCE SUMMARY.~~ 17th Light Trench Mortar Batty

(Erase heading not required.)

Army Form C. 2118.

Volume VII

Place	Date	Hour	Summary of Events and Information	Remarks and references to Appendices
HANCOURT. 62c S.E. Q8b	Feb. 1918. 1st to 6th		Battery in training at HANCOURT. Training programme carried out.	
ROISEL 62c. K16	7th		Battery entrained at HANCOURT for ROISEL proceeding thence to TEMPLEUX relieving 72nd Brigade L.T.M.B. Fire positions in the line were taken over and work in hand reconnoitred.	
	7th to 15th		During this time the Section in the line had little to report. Very few targets were offered. firing in retaliation chiefly carried out; Gun Pits & Trenches were improved.	
TEMPLEUX. HARGICOURT Special			The Section billeted at TEMPLEUX were engaged in the making of two positions situated in L5d.30.30. & L5d.30.35. on the completion of digging, Brick flooring and a Brick Base Plate receiver for each position was made, revetting according to material available. An Ammunition recess and Spare Dump for these positions was worked on	
HERVILLY 62c. E10b.	15th		The Battery was relieved and proceeded to HERVILLY. (Relieved by the 73rd Brigade L.T.M.B)	
	16th		Cleaning up of Guns & tools and general overhaul of same.	
	17th to 20th		The Battery continued the work handed over by the 73rd Brigade L.T.M.B Positions at L28a.90.40 and L28a.95.50. (DEFENSIVE POSITIONS) covering the RED LINE	

D. D. & L., London, E.C. (A7833) Wt. W609/M1672 350,000 1/17 Sch. 52a Forms/C2118/14

Instructions regarding War Diaries and Intelligence Summaries are contained in F. S. Regs., Part II. and the Staff Manual respectively. Title pages will be prepared in manuscript.

WAR DIARY 17th Light Trench Mortar Batty of ~~INTELLIGENCE SUMMARY.~~

(Erase heading not required.)

Army Form C. 2118.

Volume VII

Place	Date	Hour	Summary of Events and Information	Remarks and references to Appendices
	Feb. 1918			
	20th cont.		being the point of resumé. Accomodation of Personnel and Ammunition Dumps were completed for position L28a.90.40. a Splinter Proof for L28a.95.50 was prepared. alteration of and completion of Splinter Proof in L28a.50.30.	
			Reconnaisance of 17th I.B. & 72nd I.B. Fronts. Gun Positions chosen and arrangements made for taking over on the 22nd. Map references of chosen Positions on re-arrangement of Brigds fronts are viz: G7b.50.02. G1d.03.20. G1d.05.10. and L6a.80.30.	
	21st		Continuation of work	
	22nd		Battery moved to L10a. HIGSON QUARRY. H.Q. & one section remaining there, one section with four Guns relieved the 72nd Brigade of one position G7b.50.02. and the 73rd Brigade of three positions G1d.03.20. G1d.05.10. and L6a.80.30. The four remaining Guns were held in readiness to take up positions covering the RED LINE on "ALARM"	
	23rd		Line H.Q. had nothing to report. Section from L10a. were employed on carrying ammunition to line positions.	
	24th		Line H.Q. reported suspected M.G. & T.M. emplacements (enemy) bearings were taken and positions watched.	
	-			

D. D. & L., London, E.C. (A7883) Wt. W609/M1672 350,000 1/17 Sch. 52a. Forms C/2118/14

Instructions regarding War Diaries and Intelligence Summaries are contained in F. S. Regs., Part II. and the Staff Manual respectively. Title pages will be prepared in manuscript.

WAR DIARY of ~~INTELLIGENCE SUMMARY.~~ 17th Light Trench Mortar Batty Army Form C. 2118.

(Erase heading not required.)

Volume VII

Place	Date	Hour	Summary of Events and Information	Remarks and references to Appendices
	Feb. 1918 25th		Section of Battery at L10a commenced work on 2 emplacements in HANKY QUARRY. L.4c. and 1 emplacement at L4c 90.80. (ALARM POSITIONS)	
	26th		Work on emplacements above mentioned continued. good progress made. Line H.Q reported that on our S.O.S signal being fired 120 rounds were used. enemy M.G. fired on during the night with quietening effect	
	27th		One Officer + O.R. of the 198th L.T.M.B. reported at L.10a. line positions were reconnoitred work in progress viewed. all details explained. Defense Scheme pointed out; all details for taking over on the 28th were completed. Work on ALARM POSITIONS continued and ready to receive Guns. A Party of 20 men of the 1st Royal Fusiliers were engaged in replenishing ammunition Dumps in the line.	
	28th		The Battery was relieved this day at 6.45 pm. All Defence Schemes, maps. and work in construction was handed over to the relieving Battery. (the 198th L.T.M.B)	
BERNES. 62c S.E Q.10b.			Battery moved to BERNES for the night	
			Casualties during this month .. NIL.	
			Battery Strength Officers. O.R.	
			3. ~~GV~~ 76. 15 attached for instruction	

D. D. & L., London, E.C. (A7883) Wt. W2093/M1672 350,000 4/17 Sch. 82a Forms C/2118/14

Confidential

War Diary

of

17th Light Trench Mortar Battery

for

April 1918

Volume IX

H. F. Layton Capt
O.C. 17th L.T.M.B.

Instructions regarding War Diaries and Intelligence Summaries are contained in F. S. Regs., Part II. and the Staff Manual respectively. Title pages will be prepared in manuscript.

WAR DIARY

~~or INTELLIGENCE SUMMARY.~~

(Erase heading not required.)

Army Form C. 2118.

Place	Date	Hour	Summary of Events and Information	Remarks and references to Appendices
	1918 April			
Fouencamps.	1st to 3rd.		Battery was billeted in Fouencamps, attached to 3rd. R. B.	
	3rd.		Moved to St. Nicolas near Boves with 3rd R.B.	
	4th.		Moved to position N. W. of Bois de Gentelles.	
	5th.		Moved to Saillent in lorries billeted in Brewery.	
	6th.		Moved to St. Valery and spent night in Rest Camp.	
	7th.		To Hurt.	
	8th.		Day spent in refitting & cleaning up.	
	9th. to 16th.		Training carried out daily. Days programme including Musketry P.T. Bayonet Fighting, Arm & Squad drill, Gas drill & Extended order drill.	
	15th.		Reinforcements joined from Battalions making Battery up to strength.	
	17th.		Battery entrained for First Army Area.	
	18th.		Battery detrained at PERNES and proceeded by march route to OSTREVILLE where Battery went into billets	
	19th.		Training continued, Class commenced, description of mortar & ammunition, gun drill laying & digging	

D. D. & L., London, E.C.
(A7883) Wt. W803/M1672 350,000 4/17 Sch. 52a Forms C/2118/14

Army Form C. 2118.

Instructions regarding War Diaries and Intelligence Summaries are contained in F. S. Regs., Part II, and the Staff Manual respectively. Title pages will be prepared in manuscript.

WAR DIARY

~~or INTELLIGENCE SUMMARY.~~

(Erase heading not required.)

Place	Date (April 1918)	Hour	Summary of Events and Information	Remarks and references to Appendices
OSTREVILLE.	~~March~~ 20th to 30th.		Battery remained at OSTREVILLE, during the time intensive training was carried out. Class was trained and given opportunities of firing dummy ammunition whenever possible. Three officers joined the Battery during this period, completing the Establishment.	
			Strength 4 officers.	
			48. O. Rs.	
			Casualties NIL	
			W. F. Layton Capt O.C. 17° L. T. M. B	

D. D. & L., London, E.C.
(A7833) Wt. W803/M1672 350,000 4/17 Sch. 52a Forms/C/2118/14

Confidential

War Diary

of

17th Light Trench Mortar Battery

for

May 1918

Volume IX.

K.H. Layton Capt
O.C. 17th L.T.M.B.

Sheet I

Army Form C. 2118.

Instructions regarding War Diaries and Intelligence Summaries are contained in F. S. Regs., Part II, and the Staff Manual respectively. Title pages will be prepared in manuscript.

WAR DIARY
or
~~INTELLIGENCE SUMMARY.~~

(Erase heading not required.)

Place	Date	Hour	Summary of Events and Information	Remarks and references to Appendices
	May			
Ostreville	1		Battery proceeded by march-route from OSTREVILLE to DIVION, going into billets for the night	
Sheet [illegible] 36c S.W.1	2		Battery marched to LES BREBIS and went into billets.	
LES BREBIS	3		Cleaning-up of billets and equipment. Training carried on.	
	4 – 11		Training carried on each day for six hours. Days training consisting of P.T. Arm and Squad Drill, Gun Drill, Lectures Gas Drill and Musketry.	
	7.		Firing practices on range. Two officers of the battery visited positions of 72nd & 73rd L.T.M.B with view to taking over those positions on 17th I.B.'s new front. Conference at B.H.Q. Battery Commander attended.	
	8		Reconnaissance of Battery positions in the line by Battery commander	
	9		Training. Musketry on range from 1 pm till dusk.	
	10		Inspection of left section. Gas Drill, masks tested.	
	11.		Training	
	12.		Training for right section. Left section went into the line	

H. Layton Capt.
O.C. 17th L.T.M.B.

D. D. & L., London, E.C. (A7893) Wt. W2d3/M1672 350,000 4/17 Sch. 52a Forms C/2118/14

Sheet II

Instructions regarding War Diaries and Intelligence Summaries are contained in F. S. Regs., Part II. and the Staff Manual respectively. Title pages will be prepared in manuscript.

WAR DIARY or INTELLIGENCE SUMMARY.

(Erase heading not required.)

Army Form C. 2118.

Place	Date	Hour	Summary of Events and Information	Remarks and references to Appendices
Sheet LENS 36c S.W.1	May			
LE BREBIS	12		Taking over two positions of 73rd L.T.M.B. in NETLEY TRENCH, N.1.b.	
	13		Right Section and Battery Hd Qrs proceeded to the line. Two positions taken over from 72nd L.T.M.B. at N.8.a.87.30 and N.8.a.44.83. Battery Hd Qrs at M.12.b.25.50. Reserve position for two guns N.7.a.20.98	
Site S. PIERRE M.12.b.25.50	14.		Emplacements improved, ammunition cleaned and guns re-registered. Reserve emplacements selected.	
	15		Work commenced on reserve emplacements. N.7.a.92.55 and N.7.b.20.72.	
	16		Work on reserve positions continued, one was finished during the night and ammunition carried up to position. Gun placed in position ready to fire in front of BLUE line in case of necessity.	
	17		Second reserve position ready for use, ammunition and gun in readiness.	
	20		Position prepared for "Travelling gun" at N.2.c.95.95. This gun had no fixed position but travelled along the Bde	

W. Layton Capt
O.C. 17th L.T.M.B.

D. D. & L., London, E.C. (A7883) Wt. W809/M1672 350,000 4/17 Sch. 52a Forms/C/2118/14

Sheet 115

Instructions regarding War Diaries and Intelligence Summaries are contained in F. S. Regs., Part II, and the Staff Manual respectively. Title pages will be prepared in manuscript.

WAR DIARY
or
INTELLIGENCE SUMMARY.
(*Erase heading not required.*)

Army Form C. 2118.

Place	Date	Hour	Summary of Events and Information	Remarks and references to Appendices
Sheet LENS 36c S.W.	May			
Cite S. PIERRE	20		front and placing itself at disposal of Infantry officers, firing on targets found by them. At night this gun returned to its reserve position at N7 b 5.42	
	14 to 31		Over 3,000 rounds were fired during this period. Retaliation was opened on Enemy T.Ms at N9 c 20.75. and harassing fire was placed at intervals during the night on all trench junctions within range and also when possible on enemy Machine guns	
	29.	11.30pm	A small shoot was carried out on NORMAN STACKS N.2 b. A machine gun which had fired from that place for three nights in succession not fired from there since. Another M.G. about N.8 b. 40.30 ceased firing on being engaged by one of our STOKES and did not fire again during the night.	
			During the evening of 29th a few experimental shots (about 10) were fired at a low-flying E.A. It was found single shots were useless so a burst of six was fired and seemed to	

H. Layton Capt
O.C. 14th L.T.M.B.

D. D. & L., London, E.C.
(A7834) Wt. W803/M1672 350,000 4/17 Sch. 52a Forms C/2118/14

Sheet IV

Army Form C. 2118.

Instructions regarding War Diaries and Intelligence Summaries are contained in F. S. Regs., Part II. and the Staff Manual respectively. Title pages will be prepared in manuscript.

WAR DIARY or INTELLIGENCE SUMMARY.

(Erase heading not required.)

Place	Date	Hour	Summary of Events and Information	Remarks and references to Appendices
CITE S PIERRE	29		be close to the 'plane. The 'plane turned immediately although it had previously flown much further along our front before turning.	
			Average Strength — Offrs 4, O.Rs 50	
			Casualties — Killed: Offrs 1, O.Rs — ; Wounded: Offrs —, O.Rs 2	
			1-6-18 H.J. Layton Capt. O.C. 14th L.T.M.B.	

D. D. & L., London, E.C. (A7883) Wt. W807/M1672 350,000 4/17 Sch. 52a Forms C/2118/14

Army Form C. 2118.

Instructions regarding War Diaries and Intelligence Summaries are contained in F. S. Regs., Part II. and the Staff Manual respectively. Title pages will be prepared in manuscript.

WAR DIARY or INTELLIGENCE SUMMARY.

(Erase heading not required.)

Place	Date	Hour	Summary of Events and Information	Remarks and references to Appendices
			Confidential.	
			War Diary	
			of	
			17th L. T. M. Battery,	
			for	
			June, 1918.	
			F. F. Barton. 2/Lt.	
			30th June. 1918. o. i/c. 17th L. T. M. B.	
				HB

D. D. & L., London, E.C. (A7883) Wt. W803/M1672 350,000 4/17 Sch. 52a Forms C/2118/14

Instructions regarding War Diaries and Intelligence Summaries are contained in F. S. Regs., Part II. and the Staff Manual respectively. Title pages will be prepared in manuscript.

WAR DIARY or INTELLIGENCE SUMMARY.

(Erase heading not required.)

Army Form C. 2118.

1.

Place	Date	Hour	Summary of Events and Information	Remarks and references to Appendices
	June 1918.			
North of Lens.	1st		Firing continued from Canteen Alley gun position at N. 8. a. 87. 20 (both by day & night), & from Cob Trench gun position at N. 8. a. 60. 70. (by night only). Chiefly retaliatory work.	
	2nd		Above firing continued. Fired also on August [illegible] Road at N. 9. c. at night, & on M. G. emplacement at N. 8. b. 90. 80.	
	3rd		Above firing continued. Additional target – emplacement at N. 9. a. 25. 28.	
	4th		Retaliatory work contd. Additional target – sap at N. 8. b. 85. 90. Also fired on Norman Stacks from an improvised position at N. 2. c. 35. 10.	
	5th		Retaliatory work contd. Additional target – emplacement at N. 9. c. 16. 85.	
	6th		" " " Also fired on Norman Stacks from improvised positions at N. 2. c. 45. 80 and at N. 2. c. 35. 10.	
	7th } 8th }		Retaliatory fire from Canteen Alley & from Cob Trench. Also fired on Norman Stacks from improvised positions.	
	9th } 10th }		Retaliatory fire. Commenced to dig new forward position at N. 2. d. 00. 10.	
	11th		Registered from N. 2. d. 00. 10.. Owing to side-stepping by brigade, Canteen Alley became no longer in our area, & the gun position there was abandoned.	

JHB.

D. D. & L., London, E.C. (A7883) Wt. W803/M1672 350,000 4/17 Sch. 52a. Forms/C/2118/14

Instructions regarding War Diaries and Intelligence Summaries are contained in F. S. Regs., Part II. and the Staff Manual respectively. Title pages will be prepared in manuscript.

WAR DIARY
or
INTELLIGENCE SUMMARY.
(Erase heading not required.)

Army Form C. 2118.

2.

Place	Date	Hour	Summary of Events and Information	Remarks and references to Appendices
North of Lens.	June 1918. 12th		Positions reconnoitred for defence of Blue & the Red Lines.	
	13th		Commenced work on Blue Line positions. Position in [illegible] in front of Blue Line was abandoned. It was destroyed a few days later by a direct hit.	
	14th		Work on Blue Line positions continued. Commenced work on Red Line positions.	
	15th		Work as above continued. "Sniping" carried out from improvised forward positions. Orders received to reconnoitre positions covering the St. Pierre & the Lens Road Switches.	
	16th		Registered 4 guns in forward positions for Raid by 3rd Rifle Brigade. Work continued on main positions.	
	17th		O.C. Battery reconnoitred positions covering St. Pierre & Lens Road Switches. Registered 2 guns in forward positions for Raid by 3rd Rifle Brigade. Work on main positions continued.	
	18th		O.C. Battery reconnoitred the Village Line. 8 positions selected. Brigade H.Q. informed. Raid by 3rd R.B. cancelled. Work on main positions continued. 1 man evacuated suffering from epidemic fever.	
	19th		Work on main positions continued. Work begun on 4 alternative positions covering the Black Line.	
	20th		Above work continued. 1 N.C.O. evacuated (epidemic).	J.H.B.

D. D. & L., London, E.C.
(A7883) Wt W8c9/M1672 350,000 4/17 Sch. 52a Forms/C/2118/14

Instructions regarding War Diaries and Intelligence Summaries are contained in F. S. Regs., Part II, and the Staff Manual respectively. Title pages will be prepared in manuscript.

WAR DIARY
or
INTELLIGENCE SUMMARY.
(Erase heading not required.)

Army Form C. 2118.

3

Place	Date	Hour	Summary of Events and Information	Remarks and references to Appendices
North of Lens.	June 1918. 21st		Work continues on positions. Retaliatory fire from forward [illegible] positions.	
			1 officer (Lt. [illegible]) wounded ([illegible]).	
	22nd		Work continued. [illegible]. Some bombs experimented with at night from forward positions. Not considered a great success.	
			4 men wounded ([illegible]).	
	23rd		Work continued. 2 men wounded ([illegible]).	
	24th		Work continued especially on [illegible] alternative positions.	
			1 officer (Lt. [illegible]), 1 N.C.O., & 2 men wounded ([illegible]). Work – digging, [illegible] &	
			[illegible] shortage of officers, N.C.Os & men.	
	25th		Dug a fresh temporary forward position from which to support [illegible] 1st R. Fusiliers.	
			1 officer (Capt. [illegible] M.C., D.C.M.), the battery sergt. major, 2 other N.C.Os & 3 men	
			wounded ([illegible]).	
	26th		[illegible] 1st R. [illegible] 3 men wounded ([illegible]).	
	27th		Supported [illegible] by 1st R. Fusiliers. [illegible].	
	28th		[illegible] of the battery [illegible]	
	29th		[illegible] officer (Lt. [illegible]). 1 man wounded ([illegible]).	

JHB.

D. D. & L., London, E.C.
(A7883) Wt W809/M1672 350,000 4/17 Sch. 52a Forms/C/2118/14

Instructions regarding War Diaries and Intelligence Summaries are contained in F. S. Regs., Part II. and the Staff Manual respectively. Title pages will be prepared in manuscript.

WAR DIARY
or
INTELLIGENCE SUMMARY.
(Erase heading not required.)

Army Form C. 2118.

4

Place	Date	Hour	Summary of Events and Information	Remarks and references to Appendices
North of [illegible].	1918 [illegible]	[illegible]	The Brigadier-General Commanding made a personal visit to all our gun positions [illegible]	
			[illegible], [illegible], + [illegible]. He described the battery positions as very good.	
	3[illegible]		Work [illegible] where possible, but none of these [illegible] at [illegible]	
			[illegible]	
			Present strength of the [illegible] — 1 officer.	
			32 other ranks.	
			Total — 33.	

JHB

D. D. & L., London, E.C.
(A7883) Wt W809/M1672 750,000 4/17 Sch. 52a Forms/C/2118/14

CONFIDENTIAL

War Diary

of

17th Light Trench Mortar Battery

for

JULY 1918

Volume XIII

H. F. Layton Capt

O.C. 17th L.T.M.B.

Instructions regarding War Diaries and Intelligence Summaries are contained in F. S. Regs., Part II. and the Staff Manual respectively. Title pages will be prepared in manuscript.

WAR DIARY
or
~~INTELLIGENCE SUMMARY.~~
(Erase heading not required.)

Army Form C. 2118.

Place	Date	Hour	Summary of Events and Information	Remarks and references to Appendices
	July 1918			
M12 b 20.60	1.		Work was continued on Alternative positions. Bde Major visited positions, and found they were well-kept and very good. 15 Rounds were fired during the day in retaliation.	
	2		Work continued. 25 Rounds fired on to NORMAN STACKS.	
	3.		15 Rounds on to enemy machine gun at N8 b 80.90.	
	4.		Work continued, day spent in cleaning and re-detonating ammunition	
	5		Brigade Major visited guns in forward positions. Work continued	
	6		Work on Alternative positions completed. Work commenced on Reserve positions. 300 Rounds of ammunition carried to Alternative positions.	
	7 to 9.		Work continued on Reserve positions. 500 Rounds of ammunition carried to Alternative positions	
	10		15 Rounds fired on to enemy T.M. Emplacement at N3 c 00.20	
	11 to 16		Work continued on Reserve positions. 66 Rounds were fired during this period on to various targets.	
	14.		Brigade Major visited positions and found everything satisfactory	

D. D. & L., London, E.C. (A7283) Wt W809/M1672 350,000 4/17 Sch. 52a Forms/C/2118/14

Instructions regarding War Diaries and Intelligence Summaries are contained in F. S. Regs., Part II. and the Staff Manual respectively. Title pages will be prepared in manuscript.

WAR DIARY
or
~~INTELLIGENCE SUMMARY.~~
(Erase heading not required.)

Army Form C. 2118.

Place	Date	Hour	Summary of Events and Information	Remarks and references to Appendices
M12 b 20.60	1918 July 17		16 Rounds fired on to Sap at N8 b 85.90	
	19		Reserve positions completed. Positions again visited by Bde Major. 6 Rounds fired at enemy aircraft.	
	20		Bde area was visited by Corps Commander, who, however did not visit "STOKES" positions	
	21		O.C. reconnoitred and selected command posts for RED and BLACK line groups. Improvements to Ammunition recesses carried out. 22 Rounds fired in retaliation for enemy T.Ms.	
	22		1 Off. and 6 O.Rs attended Tracer Bullet demonstration by 1st Royal Fusiliers.	
	23		46 Rounds fired on to trench in rear of No 3 NORMAN STACKS.	
	24		Battery supported raid by 3rd Bn The Rifle Brigade. A total of 277 rounds were fired on to Trench Junction at N8 a 85.95.	

D. D. & L., London, E.C.
(A7883) Wt W809/M1672 250,000 4/17 Sch 52a Forms/C/2118/14

Army Form C. 2118.

WAR DIARY
or
~~INTELLIGENCE SUMMARY.~~

(*Erase heading not required.*)

Instructions regarding War Diaries and Intelligence Summaries are contained in F. S. Regs., Part II. and the Staff Manual respectively. Title pages will be prepared in manuscript.

Place	Date	Hour	Summary of Events and Information	Remarks and references to Appendices
M 12 b 20.60	1918 JULY 25		14 Rounds of Ammunition were fired on to junction of enemy front line and NELL C.T. at N 2 d 70.25.	
	26		No rounds were fired on this date. Day was spent in overhauling ammunition and guns.	
	28		New forward position commenced at N 2 c 65.90. 22 Rounds fired during the night.	
	29		1 Offr and 1 O.R attended tracer bullet demonstration by 3rd Bn The Rifle Bde. Minor shoot carried out in co-operation with Medium Trench Mortars on to NORMAN STACKS and N 2 d 65.75. 72 Rounds fired.	
	30		Presentation of medal ribbons by Corps Commander. 5 O.Rs of this battery were decorated and were complimented on their smartness and clean appearance by the Corps Commander	
	31		New forward position completed. 60 Rounds fired on to enemy support trench between N 2 d 98.63 and N 3 c 05.15. 10 Rounds were also fired at low flying enemy aircraft.	

D. D. & L., London, E.C.
(A7883) Wt W809/M1672 350,000 4/17 Sch 52a Forms/C/2118/14

Army Form C. 2118.

Instructions regarding War Diaries and Intelligence Summaries are contained in F. S. Regs., Part II. and the Staff Manual respectively. Title Pages will be prepared in manuscript.

WAR DIARY
or
~~INTELLIGENCE SUMMARY~~

(Erase heading not required.)

Place	Date	Hour	Summary of Events and Information	Remarks and references to Appendices
M12 b 20.60	1918 JULY		During the period under review a great deal of work has been done, and various targets in the enemy's lines fired on in retaliation. CASUALTIES = NIL Battery Strength = 4 Officers 47 Other Ranks. [signature] Capt O.C. 17th L.T.M.B.	

2449 Wt. W14957/M90 750,000 1/16 J.B.C. & A. Forms/C.2118/12.

CONFIDENTIAL

War Diary

of

17th Light Trench Mortar Battery

for

August 1918

Volume XIV

H. F. Layton Capt
O.C. 17th L.T.M.B.

Instructions regarding War Diaries and Intelligence Summaries are contained in F. S. Regs., Part II. and the Staff Manual respectively. Title pages will be prepared in manuscript.

WAR DIARY
or
~~INTELLIGENCE SUMMARY~~.
(Erase heading not required.)

Army Form C. 2118.

Place	Date	Hour	Summary of Events and Information	Remarks and references to Appendices
SHEET 44A. LENS. CITE S. PIERRE (Battery H.Q. area)	1918 August 1.		36 Rounds were fired on to No 2 NORMAN STACKS N2 d 90.77, several direct hits were obtained.	
	2.		Firing was impossible today, the weather being very wet.	
"	3.		44 Rounds were fired today, Targets were enemy support line N2 d 85.5 to N2 d 99.12, and WELL TRENCH. Shooting was good. 15 Rounds were fired at low-flying aircraft during the day. 500 rounds were carried to the forward positions.	
"	4		50 Rounds on to enemy trench from N2 d 77.20 to N2 d 95.55. Two enemy were seen running about the trench, and were afterwards seen to be carrying what appeared to be a body.	
"	5		Targets engaged today were Nos 1 and 2 NORMAN STACKS, enemy machine gun emplacement at N2 d 68.85 and enemy front line between Nos 1 & 2 NORMAN STACKS. Three men who had been working behind No 2 STACK ran into the trench as soon as firing commenced and did not reappear. 52 Rounds were fired. 1 Officer and 1 O.R. attended lecture by Lord Denbigh on "WAR AIMS" at Le Brebis	

[illegible]

D. D. & L., London, E.C. (A7833) Wt. W809/M1672 350,000 4/17 Sch. 52a. Forms/C/2118/4

Army Form C. 2118.

WAR DIARY
or
~~INTELLIGENCE SUMMARY~~.
(Erase heading not required.)

Instructions regarding War Diaries and Intelligence Summaries are contained in F. S. Regs., Part II, and the Staff Manual respectively. Title pages will be prepared in manuscript.

Place	Date	Hour	Summary of Events and Information	Remarks and references to Appendices
	1918 August			
ine	6.		90 Rounds were fired on to Trench Junctions of NELL and enemy front line at N2 d 70.20, NO and enemy front line at N2 d 70.50. Twelve air-bursts were also fired over NO TRENCH at N2 d 90.50.	
	7.		Today's target was Trench Junction at N8 b 80.95. 30 Rounds were fired.	
	8.		Enemy Machine Gun Emplacement at N2 d 70.60 was engaged today. 18 rounds were fired and shooting was very good, several direct hits being obtained. During the evening 3 rounds were fired at an enemy low-flying 'plane. Two rounds burst close to its tail after which it flew at an appreciably higher altitude.	
	9		18 Rounds on to enemy sap at N8 b 80.95. Work was commenced today on a new forward position in CARFAX TRENCH at N8 A 70.55. 80 rounds were carried to the alternative positions.	
	10		25 Rounds on to Nos 3 & 4 NORMAN STACKS. 39 rounds at low-flying E.A.	
			A premature occurred this evening killing 1 O.R and wounding 1 O.R. Corps Ordnance Officer believes premature to have been caused by bore	

Instructions regarding War Diaries and Intelligence Summaries are contained in F. S. Regs., Part II, and the Staff Manual respectively. Title pages will be prepared in manuscript.

WAR DIARY

or

~~INTELLIGENCE SUMMARY.~~

(*Erase heading not required.*)

Army Form C. 2118.

Place	Date	Hour	Summary of Events and Information	Remarks and references to Appendices
Line	1918 August 10		Base guide.	
	11.		Owing to premature all ammunition was overhauled by O.C. Battery. "Suspicious" shells were set aside and sent to Corps Ordnance Officer for Special Examination.	
	12.		No 3 NORMAN STACKS and NELL TRENCH were targets for today. 28 rounds were fired. Two O.Rs wounded.	
	13.		Ammunition, guns and positions were thoroughly cleaned today. No firing took place.	
	14.		20 rounds were fired at Trench Junction of NELL and NUDGE N3C03.34 and 25 rounds at Trench Junction of NORA and NUDGE N9A18.45. Direct hits were obtained on both targets.	
	15		No firing.	
	16.		36 rounds were distributed along enemy support line from N2b90.00 to N3A05.40. Repeated hits were observed on Trench Junction at N2b90.05. Eight rounds at low-flying E.A.	
	17.		Targets today were M.G. Emplacement at N2d75.50 and posts	

D. D. & L., London, E.C. (A7853) Wt. W509/M1672 350,000 2/17 Sch. 52a Forms C/2118/14

Army Form C. 2118.

WAR DIARY
or
~~INTELLIGENCE SUMMARY.~~

(Erase heading not required.)

Instructions regarding War Diaries and Intelligence Summaries are contained in F. S. Regs., Part II, and the Staff Manual respectively. Title pages will be prepared in manuscript.

Place	Date	Hour	Summary of Events and Information	Remarks and references to Appendices
	1918 August			
	17		at N3 c 20.40 and N2 b. 9.1. Sentries had been observed at these places. 37 rounds were fired.	
	18.		18 rounds fired on to N2 b 9.1. Work continued on Command Posts at N12 B 90.400 and N7 A 40.60. Owing to scarcity of material work had been delayed.	
	19.		50 rounds on to N2 d 7.9 and Nos 2 and 3 NORMAN STACKS. 90 rounds carried from Reserve to alternate positions.	
	20		60 rounds on to NORMAN STACKS. Work commenced on four temporary positions in preparation for raid by Bn The Rifle Brigade.	
	21.		Temporary positions completed.	
	22.		Raid by Bn The Rifle Brigade. Battery were ordered to support raid with four guns firing on to enemy front line N2 b 4.4 to N2 b 4/8. At Zero + 5 range was increased to allow of barrage being placed on Railway N3 A 00.50 to N2 b 85.80. Shooting was very good and no enemy machine gun activity took place on this part of the front. 430 rounds were fired. In the	

Instructions regarding War Diaries and Intelligence Summaries are contained in F. S. Regs., Part II. and the Staff Manual respectively. Title pages will be prepared in manuscript.

WAR DIARY
or
~~INTELLIGENCE SUMMARY.~~
(Erase heading not required.)

Army Form C. 2118.

Place	Date	Hour	Summary of Events and Information	Remarks and references to Appendices
	1918 August			
Line	22		afternoon 126 rounds were carried to alternative position	
	23		Ammunition carrying was continued, all BLUE line positions being filled to replace those used during the raid.	
	24		18 Rounds on to N2 b 9.1.	
	25		Night firing was carried out on NORMAN STACKS This was the wish of O.C Rifle Brigade. Fire was kept up at intervals during the night, 85 rounds being fired.	
	26		No firing took place. All guns were thoroughly overhauled and ammunition examined & cleaned.	
3	27.		12 rounds were fired on No. 3 & 4 NORMAN STACKS and 30 rounds distributed on NELL TRENCH; N8.b.85.95. and No. 2 NORMAN STACKS. Direct hits on trench between No. 3 & 2 N. STACKS were observed.	
	28.		10 rounds (registration purposes) fired from temporary emplacement in NESTOR TRENCH on to NORMAN TRENCH - N.2.b.65.10 to N.2.b.70.70.	
1 2 3	29.		Fired 21 rounds on to No. 1 STACK. Ammunition stores in NESTOR & COSY TR'S prepared for reception of 200 rounds in each.	

D. D. & L., London, E.C.
(A7883) Wt. W807/M1672 350,000 4/17 Sch. 52a Forms C/2118/14

Army Form C. 2118.

Instructions regarding War Diaries and Intelligence Summaries are contained in F. S. Regs., Part II. and the Staff Manual respectively. Title pages will be prepared in manuscript.

WAR DIARY
or
INTELLIGENCE SUMMARY.
(Erase heading not required.)

Place	Date	Hour	Summary of Events and Information	Remarks and references to Appendices
Line.	1918 August 30.		10 rounds fired on Sentry Post N.2.b.95.10. Command Posts completed; and 200 rounds carried to COSY & NESTOR positions respectively.	
	31.		48 rounds fired on NO & NELL TRS & Sap N.8.b.80.95. Alternative positions replenished with 400 rounds.	
			Officers O.Rs.	
			Strength of Battery 4. 46.	
			Casualties:	
			Killed. 1	
			Wounded. 3.	
			J. F. Robertson Lieut.	
			for O.C. 17. L.T.M.B.	

D. D. & L., London, E.C.
(A7833) Wt. W809/M1672 350,000 4/17 Sch. 52a Forms C/2118/14

CONFIDENTIAL.

War Diary

of

17th Light Trench Mortar Battery

Volume No. XV September 1918.

H H Layton Capt.
O.C. 17th L.T.M.B.

Instructions regarding War Diaries and Intelligence Summaries are contained in F. S. Regs., Part II. and the Staff Manual respectively. Title pages will be prepared in manuscript.

WAR DIARY
or
~~INTELLIGENCE SUMMARY.~~
(Erase heading not required.)

Army Form C. 2118.

Place	Date	Hour	Summary of Events and Information	Remarks and references to Appendices
In the Line.	Sept 1918.			
	1 to 4.		Half Battery in the Line. Nothing of note for entry. Remaining teams went out to Les BREBIS for cooperative training with resting Battalion	
	5.		Under instructions from B.G.C. experiment was carried out at Battery Rear H.Q. to test carrying capacity of Limbers loaded with mortars &c for possible advance. One gun was withdrawn from the Line for the purpose. Report submitted to Bde H.Q. on result of experiment.	
			14 rounds fired on N.8.b.86·95.	
	6.		24 rounds (registration) fired on N.8.b.86·95, & N.3.c.0.12.	
	7.		14 rounds fired on junction of NELL TR. & Enemy front line. Conference	
	8.		attended at Bde advanced H.Q. Instructions re raid by 1st Bn Royal Fusiliers recd.	
	8.		24. rounds (diversion) fired on NORMAN TRENCH. N.2.b.70·40	
	9.		19. rounds (registration) fired on N.8.b.98·82 & N.9.a.20·82.	
	10.		Four guns of the Battery supported an operation carried out by 1st Bn Royal Fusiliers, firing 464 rounds on targets already registered, viz:- N.8.b.86·95 to N.3.c.0.12; N.8.b.98·82 to N.9.a.20·82; Nos 1 & 2 NORMAN STACKS. Direct hits were obtained on No 1. STACK & Enemy front line between Nos 1 & 2 STACKS. Flank Barrage was commented on favourably by the raiding party	
J.H.				

D. D. & L., London, E.C. ... Forms/C.2118/

Instructions regarding War Diaries and Intelligence Summaries are contained in F. S. Regs., Part II, and the Staff Manual respectively. Title pages will be prepared in manuscript.

WAR DIARY
or
~~INTELLIGENCE SUMMARY~~.
(*Erase heading not required.*)

Army Form C. 2118.

Place	Date	Hour	Summary of Events and Information	Remarks and references to Appendices
In the Line	Sept. 1918. 11 & 12		Particularly heavy weather caused unfavourable shooting conditions. Ammunition was carried by Battery to replenish pits used for firing on 10th. Half Battery relieved in the Line by teams from Les BREBIS.	
	13.		All guns in Line thoroughly overhauled & cleaned. Ammunition also examined & put in good order. Repairs carried out on pits damaged by storms. Ammunition carried to forward position in COSY TR.	
	14.		24 rounds fired on No. 2 NORMAN STACKS. Battery Commander 72 L.T.M.B. inspected positions &c preparatory to taking over.	
	15.		Handing over ammunition & gun positions to 72. L.T.M.B.	
	16.		All guns withdrawn from the Line to Battery H.Q. Line H.Q. in new Sector reconnoitred, reserve positions in CAMERON ALLEY reconnoitred.	
	17.		4 guns placed at Line H.Q. under guard. Half Battery less the guard withdrawn to Les BREBIS	
LES BREBIS.	18 to 21.		Intensive Training of Battery – particularly in respect to open warfare – carried out. Teams detailed to cooperate with the Battalions of the Brigade.	

[initials]

D. D. & L., London, E.C. (A7853) Wt. W5o3/M1672 350,000 4/17 Sch. 52a Forms C/2118/14

Instructions regarding War Diaries and Intelligence Summaries are contained in F. S. Regs., Part II. and the Staff Manual respectively. Title pages will be prepared in manuscript.

WAR DIARY
or
~~INTELLIGENCE SUMMARY.~~

(Erase heading not required.)

Army Form C. 2118.

Place	Date	Hour	Summary of Events and Information	Remarks and references to Appendices
	Sept. 1918.			
LES BREBIS.	22.		2 fully equipped gun teams paraded & practised attack operation in conjunction with 3rd Bn The Rifle Brigade. Remainder of Battery continued varied training.	
	23.		Training continued, and 2 positions reconnoitred to cover LYNN TRENCH;	
	24.		2 to cover O.G.1. & 4 to cover NOTTINGHAM TRENCH also sited.	
	25 26.		Intensive training carried out. Advance formations & immediate action practices executed.	
	27.		Fully equipped Battery march to MARQUEFFLES TRAINING AREA. Rifle and revolver practices carried out. Attack in support of assaulting troops & emergency operations worked on.	
	28.		Training continued.	
	& 29.		Handed over Line H.Q. & gun positions to relieving Battery - 174. L.T.M.B.	
	30.		Moved from LES BREBIS by march route to HERSIN.	
			STRENGTH. Officers 4. O.Rs. 46.	
[illegible]			CASUALTIES NIL.	

[signature] Capt.
O.C. 17. L.T.M.B.

D. D. & L., London, E.C. (A7833) Wt. W609/M1672 350,000 4/17 Sch. 52a Forms/C/2118/14

www.ingramcontent.com/pod-product-compliance
Lightning Source LLC
Chambersburg PA
CBHW081429160426
43193CB00013B/2227